Reflections
on San Francisco Bay

Reflections on San Francisco Bay

A Kayaker's Tall Tales
Volume IV

John Boeschen

Contents

To friends, family, and long paddles.

Introduction

If you're looking for advice on the best forward stroke, fast hull designs, paddle-float rescues, bracing techniques in high surf, quick-release spray skirts, waterproof cameras and VHFs, you won't find it here.

What you will find in this book are tall tales of a weekly (mostly Thursdays) kayaking group (mostly Boomers) on San Francisco Bay (mostly in the north bay). This is volume 4 of *Reflections on San Francisco Bay: A Kayaker's Tall Tales*. Our group's been paddling the waters for a few years now, though that "volume 4" reference is a bit misleading: we've been at it two years longer than that number would suggest.

A bum knee started the whole enterprise in 1998. My bum knee, actually. An avid mountain biker, I (a) over did it, (b) got old, (c) all of the above, and was forced to take a breather from pedaling. A friend and fellow mountain biker, Sam, suggested paddling. Another mountain bike buddy, Jay, joined us at the start. We've been yaking together ever since.

Along the way, others joined our merry band, some hanging in there for the long term, others along for a shorter ride. Besides Sam, Jay, and me, you'll also meet Gristle, Wild Bill, Now-'n-Again Ben, Danny, SF Dave, StarMan . . .

The actual list of names for Thursday night paddles (yup, we yak mostly at night) is 40 strong, though we've never had the complete group together at one time. The best attended outings number ten or eleven paddlers. Three to seven is far more common. Numbers, however, aren't important; what's important is that you can count on someone being at the launch Thursday nights eager to yak.

As a group, we're laidback, keeping pretty much to ourselves. If you've got wind of us before laying hands on this book, odds are the source was one of these three possibilities:

1. You're on the receiving end of the "Thurseve Paddle Reports," a short write-up of each weekly paddle emailed to interested readers (each year's reports bundled into a single volume, four volumes currently in the series).
2. You've seen our paddling photos posted on the web. A week after each New Years, I pull the previous year's images down and start all over. The photos are at this address: http://homepage.mac.com/jboeschen. No promises, though. The way web sites come and go on the net, I can't make any guarantees it'll be there when you type the address into your browser. But it's worth a try.
3. You saw us listed as a San Francisco Bay resource in the back of *Hidden Treasures of San Francisco Bay* (Heyday Books, 2004). A collection of color photos by photographer Dennis Anderson, this is a book that wants to be on your coffee table.

If you enjoy this tome and want to read more, other volumes in the *Reflections on San Francisco Bay* series can be found at this web address: http://www.booksurge.com/.

However you came across this book, welcome! And if you're ever in the San Francisco Bay Area, join us some Thursday evening for a paddle.

1. Pt. San Pablo and Beyond

Danny, Gristle, Jay, Sam, and I launch from the Pt. San Pablo Yacht Club in San Pablo. Tucked in close to nowhere, the little boat harbor's right out of the 40s and 50s. The dockside café sports polished stainless steel trim, Formica counter tops, and red leather bar stools. Outside is a dirt parking lot, and in the small harbor are live-aboard boats that last catered to the jet set during the reigns of FDR, Truman, and Ike.

Not far from the harbor we pass a derelict pier with the dubious distinction of being the last American whaling station. The place closed down in December 1971 after a sperm whale from the Farallone islands was brought in for processing. The boat that hauled the creature was a sister ship to Jacque Cousteau's Calypso. Imagine that.

Around the point from the processing station we paddle alongside the village of Pt. Molate, the place dominated by a monstrous red brick building complete with corner turrets and battlements. From 1909 to 1919, it (Winehaven) claimed title to the world's largest winery until Prohibition permanently closed its spigots. Winehaven and the other oddities in Pt. Molate were snapped up by the U.S. Navy in 1941 as a Naval Fuel Depot. That operation shutdown in 1995.

Enough history. Now the fun stuff.

We land on the west side of Red Rock close to a tunnel we explored a month ago. Further down the beach—exposed because of the low tide—we discover two more tunnels. One burrows into the hillside 75 feet and deadends in a crumble of rock. The other one has a very different ending.

"Look at this," Danny says to me, "where do you think it goes?"

What he's found is a shoulder-wide hole that opens at the top of the tunnel's back wall. He pokes his head through and looks around. "I think there's another shaft that goes further up," he says, "but I can't see how far."

We exit the tunnel and join Gristle, Jay, and Sam on the beach. "What'd you guys find?" We tell them, speculate about the shaft's height, then drop the topic to eat.

But not for long. My curiosity wrestles me back into the tunnel for a closer look. I stare at that little hole for maybe five minutes before I build up the nerve to slither through. A chamber the size of a small one-car garage is on the other side. And Danny was right: a second shaft does climb upward at a steep angle. But he hasn't seen everything.

Parked ten feet below the dirt mound I'm standing on is the entrance to another tunnel. I slide down the loose shale to a rock floor. This lower tunnel's hacked out of solid rock, is 6-feet high and 4-feet wide. The beam from my flashlight leads me 50 feet to a far rock wall, and the whole way I'm fantasizing Orcs, werewolves, and other things that jump out of the dark.

At the wall, the tunnel makes a sharp left-hand turn into more darkness. "What the heck," and I follow the chiseled walls another 50 feet before reaching an impasse. I roll aside a few of the bigger rocks tumbled there, but no hidden passages appear. A sure sign that I should bid the place farewell.

Before leaving the dark complex, I flash the light into the upper shaft above the exit hole. The beam dims into nothingness. "I'm here, why not?" and start to climb up. But the dirt's loose, and I slide back down. Another sign I should leave. I ease down through the escape hole . . . feet, knees, waist, chest, and get stuck at my shoulders.

Squirming doesn't help me down, but it does help me lever myself up out of the opening and back into the upper chamber.

Only because I saw it in one of those Indiana Jones' flicks ("Temple of Doom"?), I slide down feet first again, but this time I keep my arms straight above my head. I'm through that hole faster than a greased pig at the county fair.

From Red Rock, we yak to Keller Beach in Pt. Richmond, chat with a friend of Danny's who just happens to be strolling on the beach with his wife, then paddle back to the Pt. San Pablo Yacht Club.

Stats

Date: Thursday, January 30, 2003.
Distance: 10.42 nautical miles.
Speed: 2.32 knots.
Time: 4.5 hours.
Spray factor: Decent around The Brothers.
Dessert: Can't remember if we had any.

2. We Meet the National Guard

An oil slick of surf scooters darkens the shadow the Golden Gate Bridge tosses on the waters around Lime Pt. Sleek black birds, they take to the air almost as quietly as a haunt of owls (their only sound a slight whistling reminiscent of the Federation's fighter planes in "Star Wars").

Sam, Gristle, Danny, Now-'n-Again Ben, S.F. Dave, and I are the cause of their abrupt flight. We didn't set out to disturb the peaceful gathering, but the only course for us (and any other boat passing by Horseshoe Cove on its way to the Pacific) is through the Bridge's shadow.

Our original paddle plan was to launch from Horseshoe and ride the last of the eastward-moving flood to Alcatraz Island, then on to Angel Island for snacks and R&R. If we lounged long enough on Angel, we'd catch the ebb back to Horseshoe. A white-capping wind from the San Joaquin Valley blows those plans under the bridge and out to sea.

BTW, the cloud of scooters spills back onto the bay once we're under the bridge and clearly moving away from the reconstituted slick.

Crossing under the bridge—a sometimes hazardous undertaking—is a piece of cake. The wind at our backs more than makes up for the slow-moving flood in our faces, and by the time we reach Kirby Cove, both wind and current have slowed. We yak in these unusually sublime conditions toward Pt. Bonita under a sky as sharp and clear as Czechoslovakian cut glass. Our only obstacle is a too-bright sun.

A mile from Pt. Bonita the wind gets a second breath and begins beating on our backs. That's ok, but not the thought of paddling against it all the way back to Horseshoe later in the dark. Reconnoitering and filling our gullets a top priority, we set up a temporary mess on a quarter mile of baby-fine sand a grassy ridgeline south of Rodeo lagoon and the Headlands Art Center. The sand on that beach is so fine, Now-'n-Again spends his R&R digging and scratching the stuff out of the not-so-retractable skeg on his kayak.

Over tasty morsels of lamb (courtesy of S.F.'s first mate), Russian and Czech beer, we sort through our options and unanimously agree on one: back to Horseshoe ASAP. It's a sound plan and we follow it . . . for awhile.

We're on the water less than 10 minutes when the wind goes AWOL again. Not long after, we spy the open mouth of a shallow cave nestled in a shoreline cliff. The low afternoon sun is shining directly into it. The hole goes in about 40 feet and ends in a small beach of packed sand. Lackadaisical water, unfestered by swells and wind, is lapping sweetly on the strand. Right out of a slick south seas travel brochure.

I'm a sucker for those slick brochures (I like running my finger tips over the glossy smooth covers), and I paddle in. If I've been told once, I've been told a gawdzillion times never to judge a brochure by its cover. I reach the sand at the cave's end when the first swell moves in. It lifts me up on its rebound off the cave wall and pushes me toward the mouth; but I don't make it out because the next swell is already coming in. And so it goes.

I'm the hungry kid with his hand in the cookie jar, I am: I got in, but I can't get out. By the time my precarious position soaks in, the water suddenly calms, leaving me a momentary respite. I pop the skirt off the boat, climb out, turn the kayak 180 degrees so the bow faces out, climb back in, stretch the spray skirt over the coaming, and get whonked by the next incoming swell. But like the Boy Scout I never was, I'm ready this time and paddle out to the others, a little wetter behind the ears than when I wandered in.

While I've been tangoing with cave waves, the current in the straits has done its own 180 and is now ebbing against our bows. The closer we draw to the bridge, the harder the current tries to push us back. We get a beggar's reprieve in the lee of Kirby Cove, but once we leave the cove for Lime Pt. and the north tower, the water's at a full gallop.

Some of us paddle close to the tower, others further out. Doesn't seem to make much difference. Though the tidelog claims the current should be close to slack at this time at that place, it isn't. No matter where we are, the horses have stampeded. After a back- and shoulder-ache of paddling, three of us limp into quiet waters. The other three are together and 50 yards behind. Ten more minutes of whirligig paddling and we'll be a group again.

Next thing we know, the ebb's spiked up a notch and is hauling the three stern-first back under the bridge. Sam heads off to the Coast Guard station at Horseshoe. I park my boat on a nearby jetty while S.F. keeps watch on the tower. A road on the jetty leads to the other side of Lime Point, and I hike to the end. The three are there when I arrive, on the road, shivering in the dark. They've managed to paddle into the lee of the tower and take out on the rocks, then bypass the concertina-wire-topped fence to the road.

Their kayaks still aground, the three hike to the Coast Guard station, update their status from questionable (Sam's alert to the authorities) to self-rescued, and ask if they can get keys to open the gates on the jetty to reclaim their boats. In the meantime, Sam, S.F., and I paddle out to the Coast Guard cruiser that had gone looking for our buddies and is now idling outside the Horse's mouth.

The crew of four is young, energetic, and pleasantly professional (not to mention the best-looking I've ever met . . . I'm speaking as a father figure, mind you). Great PR for the Coast Guard, IMHO. If you're unfortunate enough to need rescuing, this is the group you want tossing life lines your way. We all yatter on a while swapping stories, talking the Gate and currents, and capture a few virtual Kodak moments before parting company.

So much for us. What's happening to the other three? The National Guard's been called in who, with their M-16s at the ready, escort the little group in their armored Humvee down the jetty to retrieve the boats. No idle chatter. No photo op. Just steely eyes and no nonsense, thankyouverymuch.

There you have it: another paddle in the backwater estuary they call San Francisco Bay.

Stats

Date: Thursday, February 6, 2003.
Distance: Much further than we actually paddled.
Speed: Relative.
Time: Multilayered.
Spray factor: Off and on.
Dessert: A whole loaf of banana bread courtesy Gristle and a pound of chocolate things courtesy S.F.

3. Submarine Nets

Ahhh . . . the good life. We had a choice between a gritty Jailhouse or an upscale Tiburon launch. It was a no-brainer, the four of us—Gristle, Sam, Danny, and I—opting for the manicured put-in at Paradise Cay. It's not often we're able to hobnob in such society (having been run off by the locals in a nearby hood not so many years back), and this time we took advantage of a gracious invite from a sympathetic resident kayaker, HJ.

With HJ leading the way, we paddled out of his backyard past a flotilla of neighboring sailboats, day cruisers, and speedboats into a calm bay. The gray sky—contorted into lumps and twists—had more character than the water, which was quite laidback. Rain threatened, but it was only bluster, the entire paddle a dry affair.

HJ, who considered himself a novice paddler but left all but Sam in his wake, yakked the two miles to Pt. Chauncey before heading back to his place in Paradise. The rest of us ambled on around the point toward Raccoon Straits. Not far from the point, we spotted two other kayakers coming our way.

Meeting other kayakers midpaddle midweek is a rare event, let me tell you. Our little Thursday group has become very possessive of the north bay, and my initial reaction to seeing the two boaters was "whata' they doing here? The bay isn't big enough for the both of us." But it was brief, that Charles Bronson reaction, and we talked amicably for 10 minutes about the kayaking life before moving on, the two kayakers (Alan and Ellen) to Sausalito and the four of us to Angel Island.

Not far from where we crossed wakes is the Romberg Tiburon Center for Environmental Studies (part of San Francisco State University). In spite of its high falutin' name, the site's got a colorful history. Back in the 1930s, cables for the Golden Gate Bridge were reeled and stored in a Navy warehouse on the grounds. During World War II, anti-submarine and anti-torpedo nets were strung together there and shipped to Navy bases along the West Coast and across the Pacific.

The most famous of the nets, 7 miles long and 7,000 tons, was strung across the entrance to San Francisco Bay to keep out enemy subs. Some folks claim the net was under the Golden Gate Bridge, but I recently saw an old map on the Internet showing a white line inked in between Crissy Field and the plant, claiming it was the net. Makes sense: 7 miles would be too long for the bridge's span but just about right from Crissy to the plant.

Paddle close enough to shore near the Center at low tide, you can see tangles of old steel (a) nets, (b) bridge cables, (c) both of the above. I choose (c), but that's just an educated (limited as it is) guess. No matter the correct answer, it's amazing how one person's discarded junk is another's historical treasure. Just boggles the mind.

Speaking of mind boggling, we circumnavigated Angel Island. In the process, we waylaid on the south side of the island for the flood to carry us back to Paradise. Hanging there, waiting for our free ride, Danny uncovered a slough of tennis balls, all in various stages of peel. He picked out four, found a four-foot-long branch and asked Sam to fast pitch him.

Here comes the boggle. Danny connected on all four pitches, knocked those discarded tennis balls out of the park. Pow! Pow! Pow! POW! Didn't miss a one. None of us had the slightest idea he was a stickball meister. Just goes to show you don't really know what you think you thought you knew. Life is chocked full of little surprises.

But it didn't end there, oh no it didn't. The Danny we didn't know scooped up the last of the tennis balls still in the park and started juggling them, no bobbling allowed. He worked his way up to eight spheres in the air at the same time. I swear. I was there. Cirque d' Soleil stuff.

Danny's feats aside, the evening's yak held few surprises. The only event worthy of a postcard home happened while we cruised up Raccoon Straits. Midway through a long diagonal from Point Stuart on Angel to Bluff Point on Tiburon, a white super nova erupted to our left. Blinded by the light, we sat in the water, stunned.

That light flared longer than the Big Bang, blistering our eyes. When it finally flashed off and our sight partially returned, the source wavered apparition-like in front of us: a Coast Guard cruiser. Whatayaexpekt: the dark night plus the Homeland Security Panic Level at Orange, anything—including four old guys in kayaks—was suspect.

Remembering the Dawson's Creek crew of last week who came to rescue us—but didn't have to because we self-rescued—from a fast flood under the bridge, we made a run for the cruiser, hoping for a warmer reception and friendly chatter. But the cruiser eased into the night before we could reach it, and we paddled back to HJ's, wondering what kind of reception we'd've gotten if the Panic Level had been Red.

Stats

Date: Thursday, 13 February 2003.
Distance: Ten point four two nautical miles.
Speed: Don't know.
Time: Lost track of it.
Spray factor: De nada.
Dessert: A blush of Johnny Walker at HJ's.

4. Pleasure Faire

(**Footnote**: Last week, I theorized that the submarine net cobbled together in Tiburon during WWII to protect the bay from marauding subs was either strung directly under the Golden Gate Bridge or further out in the straits. I was wrong on both counts. I was close, though: something, indeed, was strung across the mouth of the straits—submarine minefields. The net, however, was actually inside the bay, stretching from Fort Mason in San Francisco over to the Sausalito water treatment plant. Danny stumbled onto this factoid while rummaging around in the dusty corners of his Internet connection. Here's what he found:

http://www.angelfire.com/bc/sanfranartillery/mines1.html

Consider yourself well informed.)

Speaking of stuff you might not have known . . . Don, a fellow yakker we met through the Bay Area Sea Kayakers (B.A.S.K.) joined Gristle, Sam, Salty Bob, Danny, and me for this Thursday's yo-yo between Jailhouse and Nineteen Palms.

We got to chatting, and Don tells us he grew up over by Bruno's. He says the tract of homes across the road from Bruno's wasn't there when he was a kid, not much of a harbor, either. Just a scattering of houses on acreage-sized parcels. No ritzy pretensions or peacock feathers and hot tubs back then, just a couple outbuildings nestled here and there along China Camp's backside.

When he was a young teenager in the mid 60s, Don says he used to ride his bike over the hill into the park. During the summer, he'd spot young adults cavorting over hill and dale dressed in olde

English costumes, sometimes less. Looking me in the eye, he says, "I think it was your end of the Boomer generation." I can't deny it: it does sound like something an old Boomer might've done when he was younger (or at least fantasized).

Following up on the popular theme of cavorting, we began to put the China Camp pieces together—belly dancers by a big scrub oak, Shakespearean actors "to be'ing" on a plank stage, strolling minstrels, rough hewn mugs dripping mead—it could only have been one thing: the Renaissance Pleasure Faire. But as far back as any of us could remember, the Faire'd always been at Black Point, where the Petaluma River sloshes into the bay.

Poking through my own dusty Internet connection the next day, I discovered that the Faire had, indeed, expanded in 1966 from its L.A. roots to China Camp, its first northern California hangout. In 1971, the Faire became so popular, the organizers finally had to move it to Black Point to handle all the folks wanting to cavort.

It may have been during those same years that peacock feathers and hot tubs became a Marin thing. Maybe not, but it sure fits the history.

Our discussion of cavorting in China Camp nearly exhausted, The Sisters heaved their bulk into view. We were 90 minutes shy of the max ebb current—which can kick up some pretty festive water play between the old ladies—and we idled over to see what was happening. The play turned out to be a heavy King Lear and not the frolicking Mid Summer Night's Dream action we'd hoped for. Feeling pangs of hunger anyway, we left the dour play for nearby Nineteen Palms and refreshments.

The Palms is a great spot. The beach has decent sand at high or low tide, acres of green grass gambol along the strand, picnic tables fringe the take-out, and, best of all, the palms flavor the environs with a tropical flare.

Our appetites sated under the tall trees, we started up the hill next to the park to gander down a hole the local quarry's been gouging into Pt. San Pedro (you get older, this is the kind of stuff you look forward to). Before we get 50 paces from our picnic table, two bright headlights jounce around a corner and light up our backsides.

Johnny Law! We're in the park after sunset and they've got us cornered.

What happens next is unexpected. The ranger who pulls up is one we encountered here a couple months back. Actually, it was Salty Bob he encountered. That prior encounter must have set real well with the ranger because he says on seeing us up close, "I know you guys. You've kayaked in here before. No need to rush off, you can stay."

Well, now, it's not often we get greeted like that after hours in public places. In fact, it's not often we get greeted like that in public places during hours. It was a real treat. If there's a lesson to be learned from this, it's that Salty Bob's going to be our front man from now on, our PR person. We see trouble coming, we're sending in Salty Bob.

After a close encounter like that, the rest of the evening had to be ok: we gaped down that quarry hole until our need to fill it had been satisfied, the return spin around The Sisters was a frolic, Gristle and Salty Bob got lost only once plotting solutions to the world's problems, and the last of the ebb hung around long enough to escort us home.

Stats

Date: Thursday, March 20, 2003.
Distance: All the way, and not a metre less.
Speed: Sometimes a frolic, sometimes a cavort.
Time: Right down to the last second.
Spray factor: A faire showing around The Sisters.
Dessert: A bag of nuts.

5. Punta del Tiburon

Back when men wore sombreros and women did all the work, Tiburon had the fancy handle of "Punta del Tiburon," or Shark Point. We—Don, Gristle, Sam, Salty Bob, and I—paddled around the Tiburon peninsula and down Raccoon Straits to Angel Island's Kayak Kamp beach Thursday evening without seeing a single tiburon (which is good). No tiburons, but we did encounter a small galapagos of harbor seals.

The seals were very interested in Gristle, some of them venturing closer than the maximum 5-foot distance mandated by the Human Mammal Protection Act (cf. Section 2, Subpart H, Preservation of the Self-Destructing Human Species). Gristle's a popular guy, the group's only chick magnet, etc., etc., but the adulation these seals were showering on him surpassed anything we'd seen.

After a travail of brow wrinkling and chin scratching, we fathomed the attraction. It wasn't Gristle the seals were after, it was the whole salted mackerel he'd stashed away in the hold of his boat at Jailhouse. A fragrant fish straight from the showcase of a Russian deli in San Francisco, Gristle had taken great precautions to contain its less-than-sweet bouquet. In fact, he'd exceeded the scratch-and-sniff standards set by the Office of Homeland Security for Orange-Alert gas attacks (duct tape and plastic) and sealed the meal in a tight-lipped Tupperware ® container.

To no avail.

Those seals were not fooled. Maybe they were psychic, maybe they had x-ray vision, maybe Tupperware's not as airtight as it's cracked up to be. Whatever. The creatures were onto us like leeches to Bogie and Bacall in "The African Queen." Even after we landed on Kayak Kamp beach, they huddled a few feet offshore, never letting go, ever hopeful.

Big dark buoyant eyes floated just above the water's surface following every morsel of that tasty mackerel, Gristle carving it up with his sharp pocket knife, dishing it out to us on crackers topped with a homemade sour cream sauce. Melted in our mouths it did. In our mouths, not the seals, which, of course, was as it should have been. Had the The Goddesses intended seals to eat mackerel, They would've directed them to the nearest Russian deli.

Thursday eve's meal was a long, drawn-out affair, not just because of the fine cuisine, but also because we were waiting for the flood to get rolling. The ebb had carried us from Jailhouse to Angel Island, now we were waiting for the reverse current to port us back. That's one of the great perks of kayaking: time the waters right, and it's a gentleman's sport; or flip the time 180 degrees, and it's an Xtreme sport. Your choice.

The evening was just a degree or two shy of balmy, and our wait was quite pleasant. A moonless night with clear skies, the firmament was tripping over itself in delight. Jupiter dominated, the brightest point of light high in the southeast. Below the king of planets pulsed the binary star Sirius, taking a backseat only to Jupiter in lumens. To Sirius' upper right stretched Poscidon's son, Orion, his jeweled belt beginning a rakish tilt to the southwest. Above and to the right of the studded belt was yellow Saturn and, farther on, another binary, Capella.

Five hundred yards from shore in the belly of the flood, we followed these skymarks back to Jailhouse, like ancient sailors. Wrapped up in the shadow of heaven's canopy was very soothing, like sheltering under an umbrella that kept the day's fallout of jagged rhetoric and sabre rattling from dousing us. As long as the shore's lights were dim, it was all up there to see: where we'd been, where we were, and where we were heading.

Stats

Date: Thursday, 27 February 2003.
Distance: Thirteen point zero two nautical miles.
Speed: Two point eight nine knots.
Time: Four point five hours.
Spray factor: Nothing.
Dessert: An incredible date tort Don's wife culinaised from a secret family recipe.

6. Drake's Folly

It was Gristle's b'day Thursday. How old you ask? The age is in the telling:

Not so long ago, I was sitting with Ancient Bob (for those of you new to the paddle reports, Ancient Bob was once an irregular regular) at a bike-book-coffee bistro in downtown Fairfax. We got to talking over hot chocolate with whipped cream on top about how lovely and full of life women are who we've seen at the local peace marches. After a detailed discussion of their many fine attributes, Ancient Bob pauses for a moment, then looks me square in the eye and says, "Ya know, John, there are times I wish I was 65 again."

Gristle's almost there, almost reached that golden number, that's how old he is.

To celebrate his ascendancy, we paddled Drake's Estero. The celebrants, besides Gristle and me, were Now-'n-Again Ben (fresh off the plane from a month in China doing who knows what), Salty Bob, Jay, and Sam. It was one of those gorgeous California take-your-shirt-off-and-bask-in-the-sun days—clear, blue skies, low 60s—that make you glad you're here and not there. It also was a week and a half shy of seal pupping season and the estero's closure till the end of June.

A backwater kind of place, the estero has few modern amenities, except perhaps for Johnson's Oyster Farm, which itself hasn't seen the likes of modern in a handful of decades. What the estero lacks in amenities it makes up in wildlife: sanderlings, great egrets, blue herons, osprey, cormorants, terns, pelicans, seagulls . . . If the afternoon winds hadn't jostled the water, we might've seen leopard sharks (the largest promised to be shorter than 4') and bat rays (their span approaching turkey vulture proportions).

The estero's fairly shallow, little fear of drowning here as long as you can get to your feet. In some places, the incoming and outgoing tides have created sandbars that surface at low tide. In the middle of the estero and less than a half mile from its Pacific exit, I went aground on one of these sandbars. I couldn't paddle, and walking the boat out on my hands seemed counterproductive. That left hoofing it to deeper water, which I did for 150 yards, mule'ing the kayak behind me. Most of the slogging was in less than 3 inches of water.

From where I found yakable water, it was a quarter mile to Drake's Head, a long stretch of fine beach on the northwest side of the estero's opening into the Pacific. The water flowing through the 100-yard wide gap was ripping and roaring, a combination of wind, fast-moving water, and sandbars. The combined effects of these three roiled the water a good half mile out to sea.

At a first uninformed quick glance, the turbulence looks like it might be fun to rub paddles up against. But deeper reflection nixes the idea. Drake's Head is one vertex of the infamous Red Triangle. The other two vertices are at Monterey Bay (70 miles south) and the Farallone Islands (30 miles due west). In between is a thick nightmare of great white sharks.

Flooding into the pacific, the estero is a conveyor belt of organically grown groceries heading for the last checkout. Don't need any bag boys at the end of the line, either, the sharks repackaging all the goodies themselves: fish, birds, and their favorites, seals and sea lions. Low on the list, just below old shoes and disposable diapers, are kayakers. Fortunately, most great whites rarely bite our scrawny, sour hides more than once before moving on to tastier treats.

Which is why I think Drake's Estero is misnamed. Many claim this is the harbor the famous pirate and queen's favorite took shelter in during five weeks from June 17 to the end of July in 1579 to repair a leaking ship. Francis Drake had just spent a dozen months in South America and Mexico liberating Spanish galleons and settlements of their treasures and was on his way back to England to make a sizeable bank deposit when his heavily laden ship sprung a leak.

Documents from the time claim he landed at latitude 38°, somewhere close to San Francisco Bay. Mention of "white cliffs" and the sketch of a small cove point an historical finger at Thursday's estero. But none of the documents mention anything about great whites, something seafarers of the time would've been tuned into. Especially since they were making repairs close to the height of shark-munching season. Makes you wonder, it does.

Me, I think Drake touched down further up the coast, either in Oregon or Washington state. Places where there are white cliffs and little coves. Places where the great whites don't hang out. A place like Whale Cove in Oregon. Besides white cliffs, coves, and a lack of sharks, Whale Cove's other historical attraction is it's proximity to the Strait of Juan de Fuca.

The reasoning goes something like this: Drake's looking for a secret shortcut between the Atlantic and Pacific (he's already lost four ships going around the tip of South America). If he finds this shortcut, England can avoid the Spanish fleet altogether and trade unmolested with East Asia.

Drake thinks he's found the beginning of such a passage at the Strait of Juan de Fuca. The strait, however, is just an inland route around Vancouver Island, but Drake doesn't know this. He figures he's discovered the Northwest Passage. Without resources for exploration, he heads down the coast till he finds a spot to trim up the Golden Hind for his trip back to England.

When Drake returns to England, Queen Elizabeth I immediately confiscates all his logs and charts and hides them away, never to be seen again. The crew is sworn to secrecy about their movements, under pain of death. No accounts of the voyage are published for ten years.

Why the secrecy? If I were queen for a day, I'd do it to keep the location of the Northwest Passage hidden from my arch rivals, the Spanish. And when I'm eventually pressed to release the papers, I'd doctor them up to further confuse the issue.

But don't take my word for it. I'd make a lousy buccaneer and a worse queen.

Stats

Date: Thursday, 6 March 2003.
Distance: Seven point eight one nautical miles.
Speed: One point nine five knots.
Time: Four hundred twenty-four years.
Spray factor: A little.
Dessert: Birthday cupcakes, chocolate ginger snaps, and fresh strawberries in a dunking sauce with powdered sugar.

7. Surfing Under Hwy 101

The problem is all inside your head she said to me . . .
She said it's really not my habit to intrude
Furthermore
I hope my meaning won't be lost or misconstrued
But I'll repeat myself at the risk of being crude
There must be fifty ways to leave your lover
Fifty ways to leave your lover

— "Fifty Ways to Leave Your Lover," Paul Simon, 1975

Paul Simon calculated at least 50 ways to leave your lover. I figure you can come up with at least as many reasons to leave a good paddle. But ours aren't as mundane as "just slip out the back, Jack" or "make a new plan, Stan." No sireee, we're creatures of high-tech, and our reasons to bail from a yak are grounded in scientific principle.

Here're a few examples from scientifically credible Internet sites that could tilt you away from paddling when conditions are iffy:

Winds seem too belligerent:
http://sfports.wr.usgs.gov/cgi-bin/wind/windbin.cgi

Currents are moving too quick and in the wrong direction:
http://sfports.wr.usgs.gov/cgi-bin/CurrTide.cgi

Tides are too high or too low:

http://sfports.wr.usgs.gov/cgi-bin/WindTide.cgi

Earthquake-caused Tsunamis could roll in:
http://quake.usgs.gov/recenteqs/Maps/122-38.htm

An always-better view on stormy conditions:
http://sv.berkeley.edu/view/index.html

The fog looks too thick:
http://www.sfgate.com/weather/fogsideclose.shtml

Wild ocean surf might wreck havoc:
http://www.surfpulse.com/cam.shtml

An animated forecast of trouble:
http://facs.scripps.edu/surf/images/maps/ganimnep.gif

All of the above, only in tiny print:
http://iwin.nws.noaa.gov/iwin/ca/discussion.html

If you'd checked any of these sites before Thursday's paddle, you would've been inclined to recline on your favorite couch. Fortunately, four of us—Now-'n-Again Ben, Danny, Gristle, and I—forgot to check our computers and went paddling.

Now, I'll be the first to admit that conditions on the bay were a bit perplexing—not exactly disastrous, but definitely thought provoking—and that we did paddle back into Corte Madera Creek, past our original launch site, and up the waterway, but in the most laidback conditions. Whether we had stumbled into the sleepy eye of the evening's storm or the Goddesses had upgraded our karma a full lumen, conditions couldn't've been better.

I tend toward believing our karma was elevated to sublime because what happened next has no scientific explanation, no web sites to explain it. We'd just finished a snack on shore and had started back to the dock two miles upstream. Paddling against the max flood current, we were able to make headway, in part, because the wind was only vapor.

Then a bluster whipped up out of nowhere. It was a nasty, tree-bending, roof-ripping, window-rattling, sign-twisting, uproarious bluster. Now comes the karma connection: that cantankerous wind was directly behind us. Imagine that. Directly behind us! We blew past the current like hot maple syrup down a stack of blueberry pancakes. It was a most delicious experience.

And it only got sweeter. The further we went, the higher the waves fetched by the wind. At the dock, just a few strokes from Highway 101's crossing of the creek, the windwaves were "lean back, close your eyes, and hope you don't pearl" steep, the same kind that usually Maytag me when I'm heading into a beach. But we weren't heading into a beach, we were surfing under Highway 101 with nothing but water in front of our bows.

And so it went. BTW, anyone need an extra Internet connection?

Stats

Date: Thursday, 13 March 2003.
Distance: Six point zero eight nautical miles.
Speed: Faster than Aunt Jemima.
Time: Sublime.
Spray factor: That, too.
Dessert: A hefty wind at our backs.

8. Titanic

There's a new yak in our fleet: Gristle's just finished a wood-framed, nylon-covered, three-holed, made-from-scratch baidarka. Thursday was its maiden voyage.

Been a while since anyone's seen a boat like this in our neck of the slough. I imagine the last time might've been between the late 1700s and the 1860s when Russians shanghaied Aleuts to paddle their baidarkas along the west coast for the pricey pelts of seals, sea lions, and sea otters. Maybe not even then: I've only heard mention of single- and double-holers in the history books, not triples. But whataiknow?

An Aleut baidarka was a whalebone and driftwood frame covered with sealskin. Gristle's is a bit higher tech than that . . . but not much. His is a framework of thin wood ribs lashed together with twine and covered in rip-proof (so they say) nylon.

Being the boat's first dunking, we (Jay, Gristle, Danny, Salty Bob, Sam, Wild Bill, and I) did a tea-party dock launch in the calm waters of Corte Madera Creek following a champagne christening. Mellowed by the spirited ceremony and benign conditions, shoehorning myself through the boat's tight cockpit wasn't as fretful as I'd imagined.

First time out, Gristle opted for a two-stroker rather than a three: he sat upfront in the captain's seat and I in the outback. In the middle we stashed the evening's food and drink instead of a third paddler. Being of a conservative nature, I suggested we head up the creek where the shores were comfortably close and the water patently civilized.

What a surprise that boat was. No matter how relaxed our stroke, we'd pull away from the others. Only Sam hung with us. But I've got to be honest about this: even Sam—probably the strongest paddler in our group—hollered "mercy" after a while. That's how fast Gristle and I were moving. Chaps my lips just thinking about it.

At the top of the creek, we turned back, which was no small chore. A little shorter than the Titanic, but rudderless, that baidarka begged elbow room to swing around, Gristle sweeping a broad stroke upfront and me doing a heavy-handed stern rudder from the outback. For smaller course corrections, the going was much easier, the two of us leaning the boat to one side or the other while we paddled.

Up the creek, we'd been going against the current. Now that we were with it, we flew across the water like a smooth-bottomed stone on a mission. Before skipping out the channel, we agreed to regroup at San Quentin Beach for dinner.

Past Larkspur ferry terminal just before the prison, a catamaran ferry approached us. The tide had been ebbing, the water level was low, and the ferry's wake was big, steep, and breaking. We swung the baidarka around to paddle into the break.

If you ever have the opportunity to yak a double or a triple, take the back seat. That first wake tidal-waved over Gristle's head, drenching him to the core. Not a drop reached me in the outback. The same for the second wave. And the third. And the fourth. Back is better.

The baidarka, unlike Gristle, came through the pounding unruffled. But here the story changes course. To give you a foretaste of what's to come, I'll sing a song (hum along if you like):

> *Oh, they built the ship Titanic, to sail the ocean blue*
> *And they thought they had a ship that the water wouldn't go through*
> *But the good Lord raised His hand, said the ship would never land.*
> *It was sad when the great ship settled on the bottom sand.*

To me, the moment of reckoning felt like someone's thumb pushing in and dragging along the outside of the baidarka. Not long after, water started sloshing over my heels. Then around my ankles.

"Hey, Gristle, I think we sprang a leak. You feel any water?"

He answers "yes" and the salt water's halfway up my calf and climbing fast. The closest land is directly below a prison guard tower 100 yards away.

"Is it a Yellow or an Orange Panic Alert today?"

"Orange," says Gristle.

That cancels landing below the guard tower, they've probably got orders to shoot anything bigger than a red snapper close to the prison. Fortunately, a small stretch of sand is nearby—just outside prison property—and we founder for that. "Fast" is no longer in our lexicon, the water's up to my waist, and I'm having second and third thoughts when the hull scrapes bottom.

Lugging the bay-filled baidarka to shore's a chiropractic appointment the next day. The boat dumped of the ebbing tide and flipped over, we hunt down the hole. What we find is a 6"-long rip along the side of the hull between the bow and the captain's seat. It's a clean slice, not ragged at all. Something a knife, a barnacle, or the sharp edge of a shell might do. Maybe a large thumbnail.

Beached but not down and out, we salvage the evening with fine food and spirits. Gristle cell-phones his First Mate, who shows up at San Quentin with his truck just in time for dessert.

Stats:

Date: Thursday, 20 March 2003.
Distance: Most of the way.
Speed: Quick.
Time: Four point five hours.
Spray factor: Not much.
Dessert: Fresh strawberries and chocolate-covered cookies.

9. Starry Night

"What's that light winking on and off to the northwest?"

Gristle and I were yakking in the Titanic, patched after last week's scuttling and very sea-worthy. Next to us were Sam and StarMan. Amidst friendly bursts of testosterone-driven sprints to the evening's final take-out, we'd rest and StarMan would regale us with tasty tidbits of heavenly lore.

A throwback to Ptolemy, I found it all very interesting, but—if the truth be known—very confusing.

"That's the constellation Canis Major," says StarMan, pointing at the southwestern horizon. "See, if you connect the dots, it looks like a dog. The bright star there, that's Sirius, it's the dog's head."

I tried connecting the dots, but all I got was a headache. Way too many dots to mess with.

"To the dog's right is Orion," gestures StarMan. "It's easy to spot because it's gotta bright belt."

Sure enough, I spotted the belt and, after much squinting, made out the rest of the hunter. His shield. His raised sword. His knobby knees. StarMan rattled off Orion's stars, but I can only remember one: Betelgeuse. Betelgeuse was Michael Keaton's character in the movie "Beetlejuice." Unforgettable, that movie.

A neighboring and third constellation, Taurus, made a neat package of the three. "The bull," says StarMan, "is galloping toward the hunter's shield. His dog is behind him and growling."

A cute tale to remember the three constellations by. But that's not what brought it all home for me. Most of the bull's head is shaped from a cluster of stars known as the Hyades. When I was a young man, I was told that if I didn't mend my ways, I was going straight to Hades (close enough). Now I know where I'm heading, and that's no b . . .

StarMan dished up a lot of tidbits, most of which I've already forgotten. A shame, too, because connecting the dots can make night-time navigating easier. Those dots are always up there, a regular roadmap.

Which isn't absolutely true. Around the time StarMan was enlightening us, a VW-sized heavenly dot did a preemptive strike some distance away on a Chicago suburb, punching holes in roofs and denting SUVs. A spokesman for the U.S. Strategic Command in Omaha, Nebraska, was quoted as saying, "For me, it's a dream come true. I always tell my wife that when I die, I hope I get hit in the head by a meteorite flying through the roof."

Weird.

That light winking on and off on the northwestern horizon? A star? A meteorite? A heavenly dot? Nope. Jay, the sly speedster, went into stealth mode at our first rest-and-lecture stop and sprinted nonstop to Jailhouse by himself. We thought he was behind us chatting up the others (Danny, Salty Bob, and Archi—a guest paddler from San Carlos). The twinkling light was Jay at Jailhouse signaling he wasn't where we thought he was, which is exactly where he wanted to be.

The paddle's first half was less stop-and-go than the second. We launched from Jailhouse into a building flood with a strong wind smacking our backs. Gusts against the flood made for some pretty good surfing, but Gristle and I got very little of it. Either the Titanic was too long or we didn't know what we were doing. It really is a long boat.

We made one stop at HJ's waterfront house before dining. He was home, and we chitchatted a while, pointing out the merits of joining us, but he declined. From HJ's, we yakked to the fringes of Paradise where we feasted on the beach: roast chicken, freshly baked breads, exotic beers, cheeses, fruit, nuts, wine . . .

When Gristle and I disembarked the Titanic, we miscued our moves and I flubbed a backwards half-gainer into the bay from the outback. Wet and wind-chilled, a bonfire seemed appropriate. Signaling their approval, the Goddesses had a jumble of driftwood waiting for us on the beach.

That fire and the food and drink were part-and-parcel of a fine outing. At our launch from Jailhouse earlier in the evening, we'd christened Salty Bob's just-finished skin-covered baidarka (the third in the fleet). A real workhorse of a boat, Salty Bob strapped a length of PVC tubing to the boat's deck and paddled out to mark the site of the Titanic's demise last week. The culprit: a rusted pipe poking up from the bay floor. After Salty Bob slid the PVC tube over the steel pipe's jagged end, we set off on our paddle.

Stats

Date: Thursday, 27 March 03.
Distance: Six point nine five nautical miles.
Speed: One point seven four knots.
Time: Four hours.
Spray factor: Heavy in the capt.'s seat, light in the outback.
Dessert: Orange slices with goat cheese.

10. Dark Sky Week

Gristle, SF Dave, Sam, Danny, and I paddled back to our launch site at Pt. San Pablo Yacht Harbor from Red Rock in splendid darkness. The real estate between Red Rock and Pt. San Pablo—had we been able to see it in the dark—is home to the Pt. Molate Naval Fuel Depot, the Winehaven "castle," and a whale processing plant.

The fuel depot was decommissioned in the late 90s, Winehaven—once the world's largest winery and built to look like a red brick castle—capped its casks in 1919 with Prohibition, and the whale processing plant rendered its last whale in 1971. Hardly a light gleamed ashore.

Which is as it should have been, especially since this past week (April 1 to April 8) was National Dark Sky Week. A novel concept, NDSW: douse outdoor lights so you can see the nighttime sky. I must admit that not too many north bay folks took NDSW to heart . . . a bright halo of light circled the bay like a ring of fuzzy hair on a freshly tonsured monk. But not here.

With just a sliver of interfering moonlight, the sky was ours. For a split second. I'd just caught a glimpse of Jupiter tucked high up in Cancer when the clouds moved in. I shouldn't complain. I really shouldn't: rain and wind were predicted for Thursday evening, but they didn't cut loose until after midnight, leaving us perfect paddling conditions in the early evening.

But I'll complain, anyway. After listening to StarMan's eulogy to the heavens last Thursday, I went home determined to learn more. I got one of those plastic "Planispheres," you know the kind, spin its outer edge to a date and time and the nighttime sky appears in an inner plastic window. I found sites on the Internet, too, that explained the heaven's astronomy, physics, chemistry, history, mythology . . . I was ready for this Thursday. I really was.

Then the clouds invaded, and with StarMan a no-show, we didn't have anyone to talk us through the haze. Bummer.

The darkness between Red Rock and Pt. San Pablo continued around the point and extended beyond the yacht harbor. An exemplary evening for yakking, SF, Danny, and I continued a black mile past the harbor toward the Chevron refinery.

An interesting place, the refinery. Invisible from nearly everywhere but the water, my first impression was a space station Isaac Asimov or Kilgore Trout might've dreamt up for one of Jupiter's moons. Where darkness once ruled, bright light had staged a coup.

Dramatic pencil-thin towers of yellow lights climbed from the shore, some measurable in meters, the height of others beyond metric guesses. We would've hung around longer, explored more, but a squeeze of unease wrapped around us tighter than our sprayskirts. Poking around an oil refinery in the dark in kayaks uninvited could be misconstrued in the current political climate, so we headed back to the yacht harbor and our transport home.

I paddled Thursday evening expecting to see stars, but didn't (unless you count the space station). On the other hand, I didn't expect to see more than one skin-covered baidarka (Gristle's), but I did.

After landing on Red Rock midway through our paddle, a fellow in a single baidarka yakked up to us. Though both his and Gristle's boats are skeletal frames wrapped in nylon, they're quite different in appearance (one hole vs. three holes aside). Gristle's boat is more Greenland'ish in appearance: a slightly deeper, rounded hull with a foredeck that curves up gently to a bow with more volume.

The other boat had a more conventional Aleut design: narrower with a linear deck ending in a traditional baidarka's knitting-needle-thin two-pronged bow. The paddler, Steve, was an out-of-work steel jobber, which might've explained his aluminumtubed frame (traditional baidarkas, like Gristle's, were wood lashed together with twine). Steve's boat also had a rudder, which traditional Aleut baidarkas didn't (Gristle's is rudderless, too).

Soooo . . . now you know more about baidarkas and Greenland kayaks than you'd probably care to. Might make for good conversation at your next cocktail party, though.

Stats

Date: Thursday, 3 April 2003.
Distance: Eight point six eight nautical miles.
Speed: One point nine two knots.
Time: Four point five hours (includes one hour feasting on Red Rock while we waited for the ebb to slow for an easier return paddle).
Spray factor: A little.
Dessert: Both Gristle's and SF's first mates cooked up a stomach-full of sweet cookies.

11. Gewgaws

It was a night for gewgaws . . . for boys' toys.

I've had this slick little VHF marine radio for two years and haven't dialed past the weather channels. Salty Bob's got a VHF, too, and we finally got our frequencies in sync to communicate.

VHF's come in real handy, for instance, when the pod balkanizes into smaller groups. "Scuttlebutt, this is Salty Bob. I'm paddling with Danny and Wild Bill. Are the others with you? Over."

"Salty Bob, this is Scuttlebutt. I'm with Now-'n-Again, Gristle, and Sam. Isn't Arch with you? Over." ("Over" isn't necessary, but it's cool.)

"Scuttlebutt, that's a negative. Over."

"He must be between groups. I saw him right after leaving you guys. Over."

And so on.

Loaded with microcircuitry, my VHF's not much bigger than a pack of playing cards, can scan through a fistful of selected channels, download its settings to another willing VHF, and memorize the last number I punched in. Pretty spiffy. In spite of this, it's not an arrogant machine. In fact, it's quite humble, it's behavior harking back to the days of Marconi and Edison.

Remember reading about that long-ago time in sixth-grade science? When two-way communications was actually a party line that played host to the entire neighborhood (we call that "conference calling" now and pay extra for it)? Forget about extra charges with VHF's: party lines are standard fare.

I'd just signed off with Salty Bob after nailing down Arch's whereabouts. Not long after, a scratchy voice clicks on my radio and asks, "Is that you, John?"

"Is that you, Salty Bob?" I click back.

"No, who's this?"

"Scuttlebutt."

"You know anything about engines, Scuttlebutt?"

"Nope."

"Man, I shoulda changed that oil pump when I had the chance. I'm dead in the water here."

"Here?"

"Yeah, under the Golden Gate Bridge."

"Anybody there who can help?" I ask.

"Nope," he says, "my buddy John's just taken his boat out the gate and I can't reach him."

"Sorry I can't help you."

"Well, yeah," he moans, and that's the last I hear of him.

All in all, the VHF worked out pretty well. My only problem was attaching it to a convenient spot on the lifevest. At first, I clipped it high on my shoulder, but then I couldn't get at it easily. The best place, I discovered, was in a front pocket on the vest. But I always shelve a flask of brandy there. Deciding which to keep in the pocket boiled down to imagining myself marooned on a deserted island with nothing but the VHF or the brandy.

I'll be back to shouting and hand signals next week.

Speaking of islands, we—Salty Bob, Gristle, Now-'n-Again Ben, Danny, Wild Bill, Sam, Arch, and I—dallied the better part of an hour on the south side of Angel Island waiting for nightfall. Sadly, the handful of stars and constellations I'm keen on were mere washed out by a moon several days shy of full. The lone exception was Jupiter, whose cream-colored Renee Zellweger (of "Chicago" fame) complexion glowed bright despite the nearby lunar beacon.

The heavens overpowered, we turned our gaze on San Francisco's skyline. The transition from solid buildings to nighttime firmament was truly spectacular, the subtle hues that delineate the stars clearly present in the city's nighttime lighting: whites, blues, reds, and the full range of barely discernible differences in between.

While we gaped, the bay darkened with the comings and goings of gigantic cargo ships traipsing between us and the city's starscape. Truly humongous vessels, they'd suck up long stretches of shore light like wandering black holes. One departing ship sat low in the water, and we wondered what could it could possibly contain, the U.S. exporting few durable goods these days.

Chasing after a train of thought approaching derailment, we seized on the idea that the ship was loaded with bottles of freedom wine. Stamped on their bulky containers would be the words "Return to Sender." Which led, in a convoluted twist of memes, to the certainty that at that very moment a twin cargo ship on the east coast was returning a disassembled Statue of Liberty to the original foundry. Hard to imagine we imagined that, but we did.

We followed the last of the big cargo ships into the bay, completed our circumnavigation of Angel Island, and began the trek back to our starting point, Sausalito's Schoonmaker Harbor. On the return yak, I wrapped my hands around another impressive gewgaw, this one courtesy of Arch: a carbon fiber west Greenland paddle.

A modern-day oxymoron—high-tech plastic mimicking wood—that paddle puzzled me. It was weightless, and its light-sucking black exterior made it invisible. I moved my arms, and the kayak slid forward, but I didn't feel or see any connection to the water.

Cruising along without a paddle, I hung in with the others. Then Sam made a break and Gristle and Now-'n-Again followed in the Titanic. Like the flu, their testosterone infected me, and I gave chase.

Stupid. Stupid. Stupid.

Once started, it's unmanly to stop. That's the law. Lacking political savvy, I saw no way to circumvent the rules . . . until the VHF crackled in my ears. The radio high-tech, but not hands-free, I had to stop paddling to respond to Salty Bob. And between calls his other two calls, I paddled slowly so I could talk more clearly when hailed. Naturally, I fell further and further behind the two lead boats. But, mind you, I fell back only because I was doing the right thing, listening after the welfare of my fellow yakkers.

I love high-tech.

Stats

Date: Thursday, 10 April 2003.
Distance: Eight point six eight nautical miles.
Speed: Two point one seven knots.
Time: Four hours.
Spray factor: Smooth all the way.
Dessert: We went to the no name bar in Sausalito for post-paddle desserts. But all they had was beer. We had to drink it.

12. Taxes and Inuits

The taxman's taken all my dough
And left me in my stately home
Lazing on a sunny afternoon
I can't sail my yacht
He's taken everything I've got
All I've got's this sunny afternoon
— The Kinks, "Sunny Afternoon" (1966)

I wish the Goddesses were a little more like the taxman. Don't get me wrong, the taxman's no friend of mine. But comes April 15, you've got to admire his unwavering, horse-blinder doggedness to get from here (where your money isn't) to there (where your money is). The man's got a plan, and he goes straight for the goods.

The Goddesses should be so straightforward when they segue from winter to spring. But they aren't. One minute they're all sweet warmth and sunshine, the next they're furious sturm und drang.

Thursday afternoon was no different. The air temperature was from late winter, the winds from mid summer. So potent were the gusts, the Coast Guard broadcast a local wind advisory on channel 16, the emergency marine frequency. But we—Gristle, Danny, StarMan, and I—didn't need to hear their advisory to be concerned: the bay just the other side of Bruno's breakwater was already punchy with whitecaps.

StarMan sensed the unease in our little worry of paddlers and, without preamble or fancy ado, sacrificed his kayak to appease the howling Goddesses. While we busied ourselves with our own paraphernalia, he quietly turned away from his car-topped yak and let the Goddesses have their way.

His boat lifted off the car like a startled duck and flapped three frantic yards downwind from its tie-down. High over the asphalt parking lot, it plummeted to a one-point landing on its tender stern. The damage was immediate: a crack jagged across the narrow tail and a foot-long split opened up where deck and hull joined.

The good news: StarMan was able to quickly repair the damage with duct tape. Even better news: the Goddesses were so pleased with his sacrifice, they immediately downgraded the wind and waves from worrisome to manageable, leaving just enough bumping and grinding to make for an interesting paddle.

Our original windless plans called for a southwesterly course (Red Rock? Paradise?), but with the tempered wind flowing out of the southwest, we followed it northeast toward Pt. San Pedro, The Sisters, and China Camp. The windwaves were munchkin-sized; but, running in front of a low-slung sun, they cast big, hungry shadows that gobbled us up from behind. The experience was unique, not unlike, I imagine, undulating on a waterbed with a young Mae West. Not exactly rough and tumble, but a nice romp nonetheless.

While an imaginary Ms. West may have been awash with excitement, her real cohorts, The Sisters, were indifferent to their lively surroundings. If not for the seagulls that roosted on their rough backs, you might've thought they'd passed on, they were that lifeless. We paddled around the old gals a few minutes trying to rouse them, but to no avail. If Grindle hadn't twitched a gull off her shoulder as we were leaving for China Camp Beach, I would've been concerned for their welfare.

We hung at China Camp long enough to nourish ourselves, then headed back for Bruno's. During our meal, the wind had spun around 90 degrees and was blowing out of the north. Paddling towards Pt. San Pedro, I predicted the gusts would die down once darkness covered us.

"I don't think so, Mr. Pollyanna," grunts Gristle, who's been possessed by an old and cantankerous Inuit spirit since building his two skin-framed boats.

"Whataya mean?" I ask.

"Those gulls on The Sisters?" he says. "They were facing away from the wind with their tail feathers spread."

"So?" I say.

"That means the wind's not leaving with the sun. It's gonna get stronger in the dark."

"No way," I say, and we continue in silence toward Pt. San Pedro and nightfall.

Darkness is in place when we round the point.

Old, cantankerous Inuit spirit: 1

Mr. Pollyanna: 0

I have rarely yakked in such ferocious winds. Paddling with the howler bludgeoning our sides is a two-icepack shoulder wrencher. I white-knuckle the Greenland by one blade and sweep the other in long, fast arcs through the water on the side opposite the wind just to stay upright.

At Bruno's breakwater, StarMan and I clamber out over the rocks and port our two yaks overland to the waiting cars. The old Inuit and Danny, who are in the Titanic and having a better time of it than us, continue on around the breakwater and paddle the last mile to the takeout.

Lesson learned: Next time the wind blows up, we're going to have lots of duct tape and do some serious sacrificing.

Stats

Date: Thursday, 17 April 03.
Distance: Half of what we yakked.
Speed: Depends which way the wind's blowing.
Time: Painful.
Spray factor: A snoot full.
Dessert: Coconut macaroons.

13. Kayak Karma

Nine of us met at Schoonmaker: six regulars (Gristle, Jay, Wild Bill, Sam, Now-'n-Again Ben, and I), one occasional (Truckee Steve), and two first-timers (Jamie and Ken). A sculling friend of Jay's wife had spotted and played with a whale for 20 minutes two days earlier on the east side of Angel Island, an event that set our course for the evening.

Having good karma is crucial for spotting whales. Knowing beforehand if your karma registers high on the kismet scale can be problematic, though. Recently, a way to fathom kayaking karma appeared on the Bay Area Sea Kayakers (BASK) Internet list. The technique involves learning your true kayaking name, which'll give you an insight into your kayaking karma. Here's how it works:

Take the third letter of your first name and find the corresponding letter below. That's your real kayaking first name: mine is "h" = Crusty.

- A. Stormy
- B. Gnarly
- C. Surfy
- D. Whiney
- E. Grumpy
- F. Cheeky
- G. Clueless
- H. Crusty
- I. Wimpy
- J. Boasty
- K. Happy

L. Stinky
M. Daring
N. Cutie
O. Creaky
P. Boatless
Q. Bad boy
R. Salty
S. Sandy
T. Puttsie
U. Gutsy
V. Soggy
W. Swifty
X. Girly
Y. Gonzo
Z. Rocky

For the first part of your real kayaking last name, take the second letter of your last name and find the corresponding letter below for your name. Mine is "o" = Muscle.

A. Kelp
B. Ferry
C. Hull
D. Bootie
E. Sea
F. Beach
G. Skirt
H. Naked
I. Wetsuit
J. Shark
K. Rudder
L. Beer
M. Pizza
N. Drybag
O. Muscle
P. Shore

Q. Water
R. Swell
S. Cave
T. Eskimo
U. Roll
V. Butt
W. Keel
X. Paddle
Y. Wave
Z. Chocolate

For the last part of your real last name, take the fourth letter of your last name and find the corresponding letter below. Mine is "s" = Bailer

A. Swamper
B. Feeder
C. Master
D. Basher
E. Racer
F. Bottom
G. Bunny
H. Dog
I. Jockey
J. Whizzer
K. Baby
L Geezer
M. Capsizer
N. Seeker
O. Surfer
P. Rider
Q. Camper
R. Bozo
S. Bailer
T. Sniffer
U. Snacker

V. Bragger
W. Commando
X. Flounder
Y. Yakker
Z. Bracer

There you have it: my real kayaking name is Crusty Musclebailer. You'd think with an elegant handle like that I'd be yakking with a passel of whales. Hah! Not a single whale the entire evening. Not even a fluke.

Maybe that's what's really at issue here: this technique for learning your true kayaking name's a fluke. But that can't be because the method's source is rock solid: "Captain Underpants and the Perilous Plot of Professor Poopypants." The book's ranked 8,055 at Amazon.com, that's how rock solid it is.

Speaking of karma, Jay's true kayaking name, according to Captain Underpants, is Gonzo Swell Dog. I can't imagine a better name. But the whales avoided Jay, too. Not only that, Jay'd just had his VHF radio repaired and was testing it on Thursday's paddle. But not for long. The slippery little sea-slug-sized handheld wiggled out of his fingers and took off in search of the missing whale.

Never to be seen again.

Thursday night's questionable karma wasn't just haunting our little drift of paddlers, either. I've become an avid backseat VHF eavesdropper. My radio's programmed to scan all the channels, and eavesdropping's becoming one of my favorite paddling pastimes.

Heading across Richardson Bay not far from the Golden Gate Bridge later in the evening I picked up a conversation between a Boat in Trouble and Potential Help. Boat in Trouble (big or small, I don't know) had a bent rudder and couldn't navigate. Potential Help wasn't sure what to do.

"Ya say ya got a bent rudder?"

"Yup, a bent rudder, that's what I've got."

"I could come out and get ya, but I don't think I could put ya at the dock."

"What can you do for me?"

"Well, I could bring out a mechanic and he could mess with that rudder of yours."

"Does your mechanic do a lot of work on rudders?"

"Not really, and come to think of it, it's pretty dark now and the water's cold. I doubt he could do anything tonight."

"Isn't there anything you can do for me?"

"You gotta' a credit card? MasterCharge? Visa?"

I lost their transmission on that transaction.

Woodgied up next to Boat in Trouble, our karma came out smelling like a sea rose Thursday night.

Stats

Date: Thursday, 24 April 03.
Distance: Eight point six eight three nautical miles.
Speed: Two point four eight knots.
Time: Three point five hours.
Spray factor: None.
Dessert: Almond Joy candy bars (now, there's a lump of pure sugar that'll take you back to the sixth grade—1957 was a very sweet year, indeed).

14. Metallica Behind Bars

Modern times are sweeping through Bruno's waterfront faster than an Electrolux vacuum cleaner. Not only has the dusty road leading to the east end of the harbor been cleaned up with asphalt, but its sidekick—a wood-framed rebar skeleton of a sidewalk—threatens to de-grime a prime muddy launch site. We're concerned, but we figure we'll be able to adjust. Somehow.

Speaking of progress, SF Dave has taken a big step backwards toward the future: he's just finished whittling his first GP (Greenland paddle). A real beauty nursed out of a length of willing Sitka spruce, tonight was its maiden voyage. Given its primal origins, SF dispensed with the traditional whiteman's champagne blessing, instead sacrificing a flask of tequila over the paddle's smoothly angular length.

From Bruno's, we (SF, Gristle, Jay, Sam, Salty Bob, and I) set out for Red Rock on a mild ebb in benign conditions. Forecasted storms yet to arrive, we were able to communicate without VHF radios or hand gestures. His first time out on a Greenland-powered yak, SF asked us to critique his stroke.

The beauty of a GP is its laissez faire attitude: it's as friendly to a whiteman's flourish as it is to a Greenlander's, though it is more responsive to the native touch. The traditional whiteman's stroke is vertical, deep, slow, and energy intense. A generic GP stroke is less aggressive, the paddle moving more parallel to the water with a fraction of the exertion at a higher cadence.

Here's the bumper-sticker explanation: whitemen do it deeper, Greenlanders do it more often. SF drives a car, and he caught on real quick.

Two miles short of Red Rock, the wind got a little ruffled, surly under the collar. Nothing troublesome, my initial response to the growing population of whitecaps was "It's probably as bad as it's gonna get; we oughta just keep going to Red Rock." My record for forecasting the unknowable, however, is dismal and the rest of the group—aware of my poor forecasting skills—opted for a change in itinerary. Our destination shifted westward to San Quentin Beach.

It was a quick jaunt to the beach. While the others made dinner arrangements on a nearby log, I took a side trip to the site where the Titanic nearly went down on her maiden voyage a couple weeks back. The ragged end of a submerged metal pipe had opened a surgical slice on her thin-skinned hull, exposing the lady's delicate innards to the bay. Fortunately, Gristle and I slogged it to a nearby beach before the weight of the uninvited water started to drag the great boat down. To mark the occasion and the hazard, we crowned the jagged pipe with a section of smooth white pvc tubing visible at any tide height.

When I arrived at the historic site Thursday night, the pvc marker had done an X-Man, vanishing into the darkness like Night Crawler. Underscoring the marker's disappearance was the music of Metallica, the band performing for the prison's fulltime residents behind the exercise yard's high walls. It might've been the overpowering walls playing havoc with the escaping notes, chords, and riffs, but Metallica's music scuttled across the water sounding a little tinny. But what do I know? When it comes to bands and metal, I prefer Led Zeppelin.

Back at the beach—a guard tower, parking lot, and several private homes removed from the exercise yard—we tried to catch wind of the band's music, but couldn't hear anything over our own symphonic munching and slurping. The only physical reminder of the event took flight during cocktails when a series of bright red flares lit up the overcast sky across the waters at Paradise Cay.

At first, we thought the flares were part of the band's performance, but not long after the first remnants of the glow sizzled and plopped into the bay, an announcement crackled over the VHF radio explaining away the flares as part of a scheduled rescue drill.

Our VHF was busy all night. At paddle's start, we heard a boater report a young kid's mayday. That alert was repeated all evening without any sign of the kid (some on the water speculated it may have been a prank, today—May 1—being May Day). We also followed the travels of a barge that had relocated a portion of San Rafael Creek bottom to just east of Alcatraz Island.

While the barge was dumping its paydirt, a freighter passed by us, announcing its destination over the VHS as Anchorage, Alaska. At the same time, a tanker 30 miles out by the Farallone Islands called in a sick crew member, his symptoms a sore throat, high fever, congestion, and troubled breathing. The fearful four letter acronym was never uttered, but you could imagine "S.A.R.S." after every other word.

A mile from our return to Bruno's, the bay's traffic controller in San Francisco requested information on an overdue chartered fishing boat last reported at the Farallones. The boat still hadn't been contacted when I switched off the radio at yak's end.

Never a dull moment on the bay. BTW, that storm that diverted our course to the west didn't show its stormy face until 11 PM.

Stats

Date: Thursday, 1 May 03.
Distance: Eight point six eight three nautical miles.
Speed: Two point four eight knots.
Time: Three point five nautical hours.
Spray factor: A few poseur waves.
Dessert: Two Ziplock bags, one filled with M&M-flavored gorp, the other Reese's Pieces and Pygmy-sized chocolate Easter eggs.

15. Gulls and Geese

We bent with the wind and change of plans like the reedy fellows we are. Danny, a modern-day Lewis N. Clark, had scouted out an ascend of Red Rock, but, standing on the neglected dock at Ferry Point, he said today's wind wasn't our friend and that we'd have to put off topping the rock till another time. Instead, we'd let the wind shove us in the opposite direction toward Brooks Island.

Standing on the dock at Ferry Point was an historical moment. At least it was in 1900. That's the year the Atcheson, Topeka, and Sante Fe Railroad ended its transcontinental crossing and built the ferry pier at Point Richmond. Put Richmond and its well-to-do Point on the map, bringing trainloads of business into the area. That was, it did until 1984 when a fire burned out the tug-and-barge business.

To be historically fair, the first transcontinental railroad to reach the Bay the Southern Pacific in 1869, building its pier in Oakland. The Robber Barons had such a monopoly on the Oakland waterfront that the Atcheson, Topeka, and Santa Fe was forced into Point Richmond. Second best, if you will, but don't tell that to the honest denizens of the Point.

On Thursday's yak, people with paddles in their hands were Gristle, Wild Bill, Danny, I, and Mad Max, who was making his annual pilgrimage to the Bay before returning to Colorado. Jay made a cameo appearance claiming business had scuttled his paddle. Our disappointment was short lived because cameo'ing with Jay was a cold six pack of Hefeweizen beer, which we quickly warmed to 96.8 F.

From the welcome little arc of sand at the point ("welcome" because it was a short lug from there to our car-topped boats), we paddled 100 yards to the USS Red Oak Victory—which saw action in WWII as an ammunitions ship and is now in a state of rusted retirement—and hung a sharp left around its wrinkled bow into Richmond Harbor.

The wind's pathology still surly, we ducked into the Richmond Yacht Club just a few strokes down from the Red Oak for a breath of calm air. The yacht club was well protected with jetties and breakwaters, making our exploration of the site certifiably pleasurable. Crenulated with posh homes and manicured gardens, the club would've made the owners of the Atcheson, Topeka, and Santa Fe proud.

Exiting the yacht club 1/2 hour later, we ferried across the harbor's main channel to the breakwater that has Brooks Island as a terminus on the east end, the west end ending abruptly in the bay. The island is off limits without reservations, a rule that extends westward along the breakwater for several hundred yards. We did a PC landing, well west of that no-man's land.

Where we did land was populated by a gawdzillion seagulls and two or three couples of Canadian geese. Hiking down the beach in search of a dinner windbreak, I spotted a nest filled with five big goose eggs. Not wanting to befoul the little home with our kayaking odors, we hiked 150 yards away before settling down for hors d'oeuvres.

Now, I don't know where gulls and geese fit into the food chain, but, IMHO, those goose eggs and the tender hatchlings we saw later may have explained the gulls' numbers. One year ago, Sandy and I witnessed a gull take down a pigeon, peck it to death, then feast on the remains. Soooo . . . what kept these gulls from scrambling those smaller-than-pigeon-sized goose eggs and goslings into omelets?

I'm betting it was the meaner-than-a-junkyard-dog attitude of the babies' Canadian parents. Outnumbering the geese 100 to 1, the seagulls still kept their distance. Come to think of it, those gulls Hitchcocked uncomfortably closer to us and our food than they did to the geese. Tells you where kayakers fit into the food chain, doesn't it?

When we left the breakwater, the wind was still in an uproar and the 1.5-mile yak to Ferry Point was a tedious backache. Danny cell-phoned the weather station on Mt. Tam and learned the mountain-top had seen gusts upwards of 45 mph. Rounding that figure down to sea level, we figured 35 mph gusts on the water. Made a short paddle seem quite respectable.

Stats

Date: Thursday, 8 May 03.
Distance: Two point six zero five nautical miles.
Speed: Zero point eight six eight knots.
Time: Three hours (two by land, one by water).
Spray factor: Plenty.
Dessert: Hot fudge sundaes at the Double Rainbow in San Rafael.

16. Eclipse

Thursday was 2003's first full lunar eclipse. The Goddess Luna did it up right, too: clear skies, calms seas, no wind. She even orchestrated the currents so that both our coming and going were downhill. Very sweet.

On the going from Jailhouse Beach, I eavesdropped on the only noteworthy VHF exchange I'd hear all evening. A deckhand on a sailboat in Antioch had succumbed to the drink and was wanting medical attention. "It's on its way" was the traffic controller's reply after a lengthy discussion with the boat's sober captain. Looking at our little baker's sixpack of yakkers (Gristle, SF Dave, StarMan, Danny, Jay, Wild Bill), the likes of such a call for them was remote, experienced drinkers seamen every last one.

Always on the lookout for experienced yakkers, we stopped by HR's dock enroute to celebrate the eclipse at Paradise. HR's hand-built Chesapeake kayak was there, under snug-fitting blue wraps. But HR wasn't. We paddled to both sides of his waterfront, hollered his name loud enough to get some window action from the locals, but no HR. The neighborhood duly alerted to his absence, we pushed on.

Luna's ebb carried us to Paradise quicker than anticipated. Bumping hulls against a quiet stretch of sand a little after 7 PM, we had two hours until showtime. The moon rose eclipsed at 8:06 PM, but the east bay hills would keep her hidden from view. We figured her heavily powdered face would emerge just before 9:10 PM, then earth's curved shadow would start to slip away, completely exposing the lady at 10:10 PM.

Time passed in food, drink, and dinner talk, all warmed by a one-match campfire of Danny's doing. Conversation circled round the coming eclipse and eclipse-related tales. My favorite featured that sly old seadog, Cristobal Colon (a.k.a. Christopher Columbus):

In 1504 during his fourth voyage to the new world, Colon found himself in St. Anne's Bay, Jamaica, with two worm-eaten ships and an disgruntled crew. The locals regarded Colon and his men as gods (amazing what a little advanced fire power'll do) and supplied them with food, water, and cheap labor.

Time has a way of moping along when you're just getting by in a strange place. Colon's crew grew impatient when rescue ships failed to appear, shanghaied 100 or so natives along with a handful of canoes and set out for Hispanola. Before they could make any headway, a storm reared up and the angry crew tossed several Jamaicans overboard, returning in disarray to St. Annes. Cristobal forgave his men, but the locals didn't, flat out refusing to continue supplying them with the goods they wanted.

Colon, the story goes, consulted his New World Adventurer's Almanac, found the info he needed, and confronted the locals. "If you don't fork over what we want," he said, glaring up at the just-risen full moon, "I'm gonna vanish the moon. Poof! Gone. I want your decision in five minutes," and tapped menacingly on his chronometer.

The locals snickered, but then the moon started to eclipse. To make a short story a bit longer, the Jamaicans panicked, agreed to give Colon the goods, the moon reappeared—right on schedule—and everyone lived in mutual mistrust and fear until Colon and his unruly crew were rescued.

I wasn't able to consult Cristobal's New World Adventurer's Almanac about this Thursday's eclipse, but I had something even better: a piece of software StarMan had emailed my way. A cute little program called "Starry Night Backyard," it let me simulate the eclipse on my computer the entire week before the actual date. I had that celestial event down pat: I knew what was going to happen even before it happened.

I had everything down pat except where the moon was going to edge through the horizon. Nine PM rolled around and—with no moon, eclipsed or not, in sight—we broke camp and paddled out into the bay. I looked low to the southeast where I figured the spectacle ought to be. Nothing. Then SF Dave shouts, "Hey, look back at Paradise!"

The now-partially-eclipsed moon winked at us from directly over our former campsite. We'd been in the right spot, we just hadn't bothered to look up. So much for our celestial navigating skills.

Errors in astronomical calculations aside, Luna's stellar handiwork was most spectacular. Cut through the haze of modern times, it did. Before long, the seven of us were swept up under her influence, howling at the splendid glow. With the lady's orange blush slowly giving way to a natural high of bright white skin, scattered pockets of howling and barking from shore joined our own.

That primal symphony and a flood of fresh moon milk led us back to Jailhouse.

Stats

Date: Thursday, 15 May 03.
Distance: Luna and back.
Speed: One hundred eighty-six thousand miles per second.
Time: Two point four astronomical seconds.
Spray factor: A bit of spilt milk on the bay.
Dessert: A solar treat.

17. Danny's Wrong Tern

Quite the paddle Thursday eve. Jamie—a wee bit late for the launch—started it off by driving into Ferry Point's parking lot through the exit. A neo-anarchistic move if I ever saw one, but personal belief systems had nothing to do with the outcome. Shark-tooth-shaped tire spikes embedded in the asphalt had everything to do with the outcome. Luckily, Jamie only shredded one tire.

Our launch into a windy bay was less traumatic than Jamie's arrival at Ferry Point. We paddled directly across the channel leading to Richmond Harbor so we could chummy up next to the long breakwater that held back the wind and waves. It was a good move, only a few aggressive swells managing to blow misty smoke over the riprap.

The breakwater—an impressive sight—is not the handiwork of the Goddesses, though the Ladies may have inspired their human charges to mimic bits and pieces of the natural world in its construction. From midlength to bay end, the breakwater is all tumbled rock and jaggies. The other side of midlength to and connecting up with Brooks Island is all fine sand and low, sweeping vegetation.

Birds love this section of the breakwater, as they should since it's set aside as a reserve. Pelicans, gulls, Canadian geese, cormorants, herons, egrets . . . a diversified flock call it home. This time of year, the California Least Tern (cousin to the Arctic Tern, famous for its 12,500 mile annual pilgrimages between poles) nests here. On the Federal Endangered species list since 1970, reserves like this one are helping the tern make a go of it.

Danny's up-to-snuff on stuff like this. He says dredging, housing developments, pollution, human encroachment, and construction of the Pacific Coast Highway all contributed to nearly finishing off the Least Tern. A sign marked the reserve's boundary where we landed, and—though the paddle had begun with an explosion of tire-shredding anarchy—Danny insisted we stick to the rules and give the terns a fair shake by staying on our end of the breakwater (not that we needed the reminder, mind you; we may be pink on the outside, but we're pretty green on the inside).

From the breakwater, we paddled along the east shore of Brooks Island—keeping clear of the posted and protected lagoon near the caretaker's house—then cut across San Pablo Bay for the Albany Bulb. We broke into two pods on the wind-swept crossing: Sam, myself, Jamie, Wild Bill, his friend Rob, Gristle, and Now-'n-Again Ben in one group and StarMan, his friend Dusty, and Danny in the second.

The first group made the crossing without incident. The second group, however, wisely took full advantage of the surly conditions. Pretending to lose control of his kayak on a steep wave, Dusty flipped over. StarMan and Danny immediately came to his aid, performing a perfect three-boat T-rescue that allowed Dusty to scramble back into a "dry" boat and finish his yak to the Bulb in relative comfort.

I've written about the Bulb on a previous paddle, so I won't bore you with details. Suffice it to say, if Thursday night's yak were an Internet search from a public library in a conservative county, we'd never have arrived, never've got through all the filters set up to keep us out. In an urban nutshell, Bulb art is a modern-day extension of Hieronymus Bosch's 16th Century masterpieces, replete with devils, ghouls, and things they don't teach in Sunday school (for a sample of Bosch's work, see http://www.ibiblio.org/wm/paint/auth/bosch/delight/).

The evening turned chill, the wind picked up, and we eventually sought refuge in an abandoned concrete water-valve bunker. Like all other objects at the Bulb—manmade and natural—the bunker was covered inside and out with murals and paintings. If a 21st Century Bosch could get his paintbrush on the Sistine Chapel, this is what he'd paint.

Adding a touch of surrealism to a surrealistic place, Jamie dialed into the Internet on his Palm Pilot phone and Googled the Bulb from inside the water-valve bunker. Lots of good stuff online. If you're curious about the place, type "Albany Bulb" in Google's search engine to see what we saw.

Hoping the wind would call it an evening (which it didn't), we hung out in the bunker till 10:00 PM before packing up. Except for one incident, the paddle back to Ferry Point was unremarkable.

Danny, our BirdMan of Brooks Island, paddled close to the island to take advantage of its windshadow. Perhaps too close. When his well-lit boat passed the protected lagoon in front of the caretaker's house around 11 PM, the insomniac caretaker spotted him, jumped into his outboard, and gave noisy chase.

The caretaker asked Danny if he knew the lagoon was protected, that endangered Terns were nesting nearby, and that he shouldn't be there. Danny answered "yes," "yes," he was guilty, but that he was just trying to stay safe in the lee of the unruly wind. He wasn't planning to stop or go ashore. Might've been the day's Orange Panic Alert Level or some such thing because the caretaker wouldn't take "guilty" for an answer.

StarMan caught a glimpse of what was happening and paddled over. He told the caretaker that Danny had earlier explained to us everything the caretaker was explaining now, but it was slow going. Some ten minutes later the three parted company, Danny and StarMan promising more than once to never paddle in the lagoon and to never disturb the nesting terns.

Strange times we live in.

Stats

Date: Thursday, 22 May 03.
Distance: Seven point eight one five nautical miles.
Speed: One point four two one knots.
Time: Five point five hours.

Spray factor: Impressive.

Dessert: StarMan's homemade pizza fired in his homemade brick oven (they do that kind of thing in Petaluma, StarMan's hometown).

Post Script: On Saturday, Gristle, Danny, Truckee Steve, SF Dave, and I chaperoned the annual spring CHOMP swimmers from Nick's Cove through the shark-invested waters of Tomales Bay out to Hog Island and back. Not to dwell on the sanity of swimming on such a cold day, but I now understand the smirk of truth in Mark Twain's comment about the coldest winter he ever spent was a summer in San Francisco.

18. Kirby Cove

Jay showed up Thursday night with a compass strapped to his foredeck . . . that's the kind of evening it was. Windy and gray all day, foggy all night.

Officially, it's been spring for over a month, the northern-bound sun colliding with the celestial equator back around March 21. But it must've been a minor collision. Some days have been hotter than Hades, others . . . well, the Goddesses are having a hard time letting go of winter. Don't know why, but that's the way it's been.

Despite the chilly, overcast reception at Schoonmaker Cove, six of us showed up with our warmest duds ready to yak: Kayak-'n-Ken, Danny, Starman, SF Dave, Jay, and I. The paddle out of the cove and through Richardson Bay to the Golden Gate was uneventful, the wind sometimes pushing at our backs from the north, other times splashing spray in our faces from the south.

A bump of excitement, however, has been careening through Richardson Bay. Seems a bit of Highway 101 road rage has spun off into the waters around Sausalito, a hit-and-run boater punctuating the hulls of at least two live-on's at anchor. The culprit is still at bay, a hand-painted black frame around the dent in one of the hulls begging the question, "Who did this?"

We didn't know and kept on paddling. When we reached Yellow Bluff—the cliffs marking the expanse of water just before the Golden Gate Bridge—we came across a threesome of outrigger canoes, each of the long boats home to four or more paddlers. They were from a club out of Horseshoe Cove, not more than a long flycast from where we floated.

We encounter folks in people-powered craft, we often cozy up to chit about this and chat about that. You learn a lot about what's going on in the bay that way. Sometimes you even come away with food and drink. Those are good encounters. This group, however, was deep into a serious coaching session and ignored us, though a few of the less attentive students did toss smiles our way. Waving goodbye almost as soon as we arrived, we left them to their floating classroom, headed around Yellow Bluff, past Horseshoe Cove, and under the Golden Gate Bridge.

Up to the big orange span, Kayak-'n-Ken had been very quiet, almost subdued. That changed once the first of the bridge's rowdy water whomped against his bow. His eyes lit up and he lit off, riding those unruly critters like Travolta on the mechanical bull in "Urban Cowboy." Born to it, he was, like B'rer Rabbit in the Briar Patch.

B'rer Rabbit, of course, was born in the Briar Patch. Kayak-'n-Ken, while not born in a briar patch, was born in a kayak, at least that's what my sources tell me. And not just born into a kayak, mind you, Ken was in the kayak when he slipped his moorings and Eskimo rolled out of the birth canal. Honest. My sources are unimpeachable (good people, but they'd never make it in politics).

We followed Ken to Kirby Cove where we set up camp in a wind-protected hollow a high earth berm away from the beach and our boats. Nestled in with tall eucalyptus and green cypress, Jay produced two bottles of champagne, which we promptly emptied in a toast to his late dad's life. It was a festive evening, with talk of family, friends, and good times.

On the return under the bridge, the bull was really wired, our boats pitching and yawing in synch with our own loud yee'ing and haw'ing. Danny claims it would've been more exciting if the current had been ebbing out the gate rather than flooding into the bay. That way, he says, had anything gone amiss, we would've been swept into the ocean rather than into the bay.

I think Danny had too much champagne.

Stats

Date: Thursday, 29 May 03.
Distance: Eight point six eight nautical miles.
Speed: One point seven three six knots.
Time: Five hours.
Spray factor: Excellent.
Dessert: Chewy chocolate cookies. Special note: For the first time on a Thursday yak, we had a freezer's worth of food leftover. The only possible explanation: the big eaters didn't paddle. You know who you are.

19. Outland

We figured we'd found one of Saddam Hussein's missing weapons of mass destruction at Bruno's Thursday evening: lying on an asphalted parking space was a nine-foot-long, space-age-looking missile launcher. Glass-faced dials, shiny metal levers, and curving hoses gave the contraption a "Terminator" feel.

On closer inspection, the sinister-looking WMD turned out to be a friend of my youngest son's retrofitted backyard sprinkler system. Casey, the engineer in question, had jerry rigged a hardware store of plastic pipe, pressure gauges, pistons, and whatnots into a hi-tech spud gun powered by a large compressor that, in turn, was powered by a gas generator, the kind you'd find in backwoods enclaves.

Potatoes on the out as WMD fodder, Casey and his cohorts gravitated toward more modern projectiles: golf balls in this outing. Cranked up to 15 psi, they launched a little spheroid 200 yards. With a head of 40 psi, the ball splashed on the bay a more-than-respectable 450 yards from the parking lot. A second try at 60 psi snapped the piston, and it was back to the drawing board.

My suggestion: on the next go-round, use new Titleists instead of practice balls and forget Bruno's . . . head straight for the closest PGA tournament and aim for the greens.

With the demise of the spud gun, we paddled through Bruno's calm harbor, out through Kong's Gates, and into a white-capped bay. Ten minutes out, Gristle, who had looked pale around the gills in the harbor, went virtually green and it was deemed best that he keep his lunch to himself and head back to port.

Jay and I followed the old codger up a quiet pocket lagoon next to the breakwater, then helped with the heaving and ho'ing of his kayak back to his truck. The good deed done, we returned to the bay, passing along the way a camouflaged cache of someone's "secret" supplies nested in a cliffside cave. More WMD akin to the spud gun we'd just seen? I don't know, but I wouldn't be surprised if the authorities hoist the Panic Alert Level back up to orange if they get wind of this find.

The water was still boogying when Jay and I pulled into the bay. It was wonderful fun, slipping and sliding through those slap-dancing waves. Ahead of me, Jay was bouncing right along, doing a lot of stern ruddering to keep a straight course. Same for me. It's a phenomenon of surfing open-water waves where your stern wants to whip around and sniff your bow. Dragging a paddle behind helps a bit, but you really can't stop the break-dancing waves from wagging the dog or, in this instance, wagging the yak.

Jay and I whooped and hollered a mile through the splashing mosh pit to Pt. San Pedro, where we turned north toward Nineteen Palms and the others (Sam, Wild Bill, Danny, and Alan—new to the group on this paddle). On arrival, they asked if we'd heard their call over the VHFs, but we hadn't, us shouting and carrying on the way we were.

This Thursday evening also was the first paddle I hadn't picked up any transmissions from freighters / tankers coming in from foreign ports with crew members ailing from SARS-like symptoms. Maybe the epidemic's on the wane, or maybe I should charge my battery. I hope it's the former.

The evening still young, we paddled from Nineteen Palms another 1/2 mile north to China Camp Beach. Hard to miss, the first thing we noticed was a wood-timbered boat under construction on the grass next to the beach. A big thick beam for the keel, we estimated it's length at 30 feet with a ten-foot-high bow. Looked to be a recreation of a boat from times past, exactly whose time I can't say. Watching it's progress should be interesting.

Following a fancy meal (Sam, taking Wild Bill's lead from last week, brought along a portable stove and cooked up some tasty stew), we set about cleaning up our mess and readying the boats. More typical of spring than the last few weeks, the wind had taken a curtain call at sunset and the water was laid down, no doubt tuckered out from all that earlier wild dancing.

Daylight's been stretching her long, pale limbs deeper into the night, a sure sign of summer to come. It's all very welcome, but it makes early evening star gazing difficult. The only celestial spheres visible were the moon, Jupiter, and Regulus (the heart of the constellation Leo)—all three pyramided close together—before the fog moved in to blot out the dark, clear night sky.

On the way back to Bruno's, Alan, the new guy on the yak, explained that he wouldn't be able to join us for the next four or five Thursdays. Seems he's flying to Anchorage next Thursday and from there to Russia where he's teaming up with a group to paddle a river that's never been yakked before. After that little adventure, the group's helicopting three hundred miles into the Bering Sea to dip their paddles in waters around a remote island.

Uncharted territory's where it's at. That's why we paddle the north end of San Francisco Bay, particularly the water north of the Richmond-San Rafael Bridge. As far as the pre-eminent kayaking group in the Bay Area (BASK) is concerned, this is the outlands, uncharted and unknown.

In the back of BASK's main publication, "2003 Tides & Currents: San Francisco Bay & Tributaries," is a collection of bay maps. Except for a vague graphic reference in a larger map, our yakking territory is not included among the area's more detailed charts.

An encounter we had with one of the locals'll give you an idea of how far off the civilized path we are. Close to Bruno's, we neared a beach where a friend lives. It was just a little after 10 PM—a decent hour—and we figured a house call was in order. Not to mention giving my friend an opportunity to offer us some beer.

In a civilized, charted world, our host would've arrayed a selection of fine beer to choose from. But in this untamed outland, our host's supply of beer had been depleted, he has none he says, and we had to share what little we had with him.

Kayaking out here's a hardship, but someone's got to do it.

Stats

Date: Thursday, 5 June 03.
Distance: Six point zero seven nine nautical miles.
Speed: One point three five one knots.
Time: Four point five hours.
Spray factor: Excellent.
Dessert: Gristle was packing the dessert, which never made it to China Camp.

20. Anthony and Cleopatra

The swell swarmed over the rock like Anthony over Cleopatra. It was an event of historic proportions that caught up Sam and teetered him on a plume of white surge. Definitely not one of those "been there, done that's"—no sireee, judging from the surprised look etched into Sam's eyes, this bit of history-in-the-making was a new experience.

The five of us (Sam, Gristle, Danny, Jay, and I) had just bobbed around Angel Island's Pt. Blunt and were threading our way through the big rocks that litter the water there. The wind was throwing a tantrum and whitecaps were the bay's attire.

Past the rocks, we all breathed a theatrical sigh of relief and strained on through the irritable water. Not having to worry about the rocks was a blessing until a lump of bay fell away 20 yards ahead of my bow, exposing the raggedy mop of a previously submerged boulder. Vacuums abhorred, water rushed back into the hole and quickly covered the jagged menace.

"Rock ahead," I shouted to whoever happened to be behind and gestured in the general direction of the obstacle. Must've been the wind slapping at his ears because Sam, who was the guy behind, didn't hear me. He plowed straight ahead toward the submerged catastrophe.

Fortunately for Sam, the bay didn't drop away and trounce him on the boulder. Bows to sterns, it swelled up high over the rock like a testosterone junky. Perched on the wave's top, Sam had two basic choices: (1) slide down the slippery surface like Anthony on his Egyptian princess or (2) capsize, fumbling his future history to the stony fates.

A romantic with a conservative flair for not rocking the boat, Sam chose the waterslide option. His was a dramatic plunge, and we stopped to cheer his escape even though he came up empty handed, no tawny-skinned, moon-eyed princess draped over his cockpit. But that's history for you; some folks get all the exotic baubles and beads while others just get tumbled about.

While we're still tuned into the History Channel, the only other island stop we made Thursday was at China Cove, California's equivalent to New York's Ellis Island. Between 1910 and 1940, immigrants to the west coast were processed here.

Far as I can tell, naming the site China Cove was a guilt-riddled effort to atone for the fate of Chinese nationals manhandled through the immigration process. While most Europeans were off the island in two to three days, the most unfortunate of the Chinese were held here for a year or more. Barbed-wire-topped fences made sure they stayed put.

Besides signage dispensing bits and pieces of the station's sordid history, a shiny dark monolith of polished stone memorializes the people, time, and place. On one side of the stone is a poem chiseled into the cold block in traditional Chinese characters. The result of a modern-day competition, the translated poem reads

Leaving their homes and villages, they crossed the ocean only to endure confinement in these barracks. Conquering frontiers and barriers, they pioneered a new life by the Golden Gate.

Pretty tame words, particularly when sidled up alongside poems carved by the original detainees in the men's barracks (the men's quarters the only structure to survive the 1940 fire that permanently shut down the station). Though we didn't venture into the barracks, I managed to find one of those original poems on the Internet:

All of us in the wood prison feel the same boredom and sadness, Here I recall how much hardship we had to endure to come thus far.

Nobody could tell us when we are allowed to get through this pass,
Months and years are wasted in great emptiness and helplessness.

On a more upbeat note, on the far side of the island opposite China Cove I discovered the answer to a kayaking question that's been bugging me for some time. To wit: is it faster to get from Point A to Point B plunging through the wave (shorter distance) or riding over the wave (longer distance)?

When conducting scientific investigations, it's crucial to have the proper setup, one misaligned variable easily botching the whole enterprise. Yaking back to Schoonmaker, all the important pieces for a first-rate experiment were in place: waves of equal height, Points A and B floating next to Points A1 and B1, and a Cyrano-de-Bergerac bow that knifed through waves (my boat) vs. a WC-Fields bow that scooted over waves (Jay's kayak).

After running the test way too many times, the results clearly favored the bulbous-nosed boat. The academic explanation, courtesy Einstein, claims that since space and time are curved, the quickest route between two points also is curved (up and over the wave) rather than straight (through the wave).

But I don't buy that explanation. Einstein never kayaked; what'd he know?. Here's the real reason: the fool going through the wave is too busy choking down salt water to paddle a straight line.

Ahhh, if only more of life's problems could be so simple, even if they're not straightforward.

Stats

Date: Thursday, 12 June 03.
Distance: Nine point five five two nautical miles.
Speed: Two point seven three zero knots.
Time: Three point five hours.
Spray factor: Unruly.
Dessert: I'm on a sugar- and processed-food-free diet (only two more weeks to go) and limited dessert to pan-fried mahi mahi.

21. Presidential Candidate

After a typical put-in, we rarely know where we're heading once the water starts to drip off our paddles. This Thursday was different.

The Tuesday before our Thursday launch, Sam, a politically savvy yaker, says we ought to stop at the Larkspur Ferry Terminal. "We gotta be there by 6 PM," he says.

"How come?" I say.

"'Cause," says Sam, "former Vermont Governor Howard Dean's coming in on the 6:05 ferry from San Francisco to do a little presidential campaigning."

A chance to showoff our civic mindedness, we (Sam, Jamie, Zeke-the Younger, Gristle, StarMan, Danny, and I) launch from placid Corte Madera Creek at 5:15 PM and work our way against a mild flood current a half mile to the ferry terminal. Designed for big boats, the terminal has little in the way of docking facilities for kayaks. But that's ok because kayaks, being on the low end of high tech, can go places high tech can't fathom.

Sandwiched between the south end of the terminal's black heatsink of a parking lot and Corte Madera's cool creek is a small, shallow slog of marshland. We follow a narrow waterway between the tule grass and pickleweed to the edge of the parking lot and quietly beach the boats on a slope of succulent, shiny green ice plant.

The boats high and dry, we traipse over to the terminal's outdoor waiting area. Before we can set foot on the smooth concrete platform, a bridge-district official comes scurrying up to Sam and says, "You can't be waving that sign around here." Sam's lugging a handmade sign left over from a spring peace rally. Its political meaning is clear, though its words tend more toward the weekend gardener. Something to do with trimming back shrubs.

Not wanting to make a fuss, Sam makes like Corte Madera Creek and placidly takes the sign back to his boat and stores it away. In the meantime, Gristle wanders up close to where Dean's ferry is going to dock. Must've been his colorful rubber outfit or the water puddling around his mukluks because a second bridge-district official spots him and moves in for an encounter.

"What's up?" asks Gristle.

"I don't know," says the official, "but you'll have to move back until I can think of something."

Gristle backpaddles ten yards and disappears into the crowd of 80 people who've gathered to greet Dean. At about the same time, a ferry-district official approaches and asks Gristle about his encounter with the bridge-district official. Gristle tells all to the ferry-district official. The official looks mildly perplexed, shakes his head, and mumbles something about politics and the bridge district before moving on.

At exactly 6:05 PM, the ferry docks. Dean and his small entourage are the last off the passenger boat. Dean's a short guy wearing a white shirt, open at the collar, no tie, sleeves rolled up. His gestalt . . . his bearing . . . remind me of old blue eyes, Paul Newman.

"Not Paul Newman," says Gristle, "Richard Dreyfuss. He reminds me of Richard Dreyfuss. That's the guy who helped Roy Schneider put Jaws away. I think Dean's our man. I think he can do it." Short pause. "Of course, Senator Kerry's looking pretty good, too. I really like his energy plan, particularly the part about hydrogen power." (Gristle's speculated a chunk of his retirement funds into hydrogen power.) "Yup, I think Kerry may give Dean a run for his money."

Dean speaks and gesticulates all the right things to this liberal Marin crowd: universal healthcare, good public schools, a balanced budget, social security, jobs, and so forth. Lots of cheering and picture taking. Sadly, while all this is going on, Dean's 17-year-old son, Paul, and four buddies from the high school hockey team are sneaking into a Vermont country club to liberate the bar of certain libations.

The next day we learn Dean has taken a break from his stumping and is going home to deal with the misadventure. I like that—a family man not letting politics get in the way of hearth and home. I think it'll all turn out ok, too: I've heard rumors the Deans may enroll the boy in the same treatment program the Bush girls are in.

Small world, isn't it.

Our civic capacity for politicking near to overflowing, the seven of us launch back into Corte Madera Creek and set course for 19 Palms. Half way across the open stretch of water north of the Richmond-San Rafael Bridge, we waffle. The evening, starting out like a well-behaved Pollyanna, has suddenly transformed her naïve self into a rowdy dancehall diva, flouncing this way and that with lots of blustery breathing.

Chard Island is less than a mile away, and we alter course. In the lee of the island, we agree to burn off a few more calories and circumnavigate the rock before putting in for dinner. Skirts are still flying on the windward side, however, and we barely make it around.

In the narrow channel between Chard and Buckwheat, we meet up with a small fishing boat. In idle chit chat with the vessel's captain, we discover our catch is more substantial than his and invite him and his family to dine with us on Chard. He graciously declines, and we proceed to dinner.

Ours is an international meal: fresh salmon, sushi, fried pork, chicken flautas, dim sum, strawberries, custard pie, Swiss chocolate, and some of the same beverages Paul Dean may have been looking for. The evening is long and leisurely, in part to properly ingest our meal, but also to give the gyrating dancehall divas time to wind down, which they do just before 10 PM. We take to the water after their final curtain call and are back at Corte Madera Creek just after 11 PM.

Stats

Date: Thursday, 19 June 03.
Distance: Six point nine four seven nautical miles.
Speed: One point one five eight knots.
Time: Six hours.
Spray factor: Just what you'd expect on the campaign trail.
Dessert: Boy, did I fall off the sugar wagon. I'm now into my second week of trying to avoid sugar-spiked foods and have not fared well, Thursday evening being a prime example. My downfall were the custard pies, each sweetly filled, round aluminum tin just big enough to fit into my open maw. I've been worrying the problem since and have come up with a solution. My solution is Ken Lay. Remember him? The CEO of Enron who had everything, but still felt compelled to gobble up more? From now on, whenever I covet sugar, I'm going to visualize Ken Lay and, hopefully, lose my appetite. Wish me luck.

22. Summer Triangle

Everything that heard (Orpheus) play,
even the billows of the sea,
hung their heads, and then lay by.
Shakespeare, *Henry VIII*, 1612-1613

Orpheus was the Bruce Springsteen of the antiquities. Whenever he strummed his lyre, wild beasts and fans alike swooned into a collective stupor. The musician's fame was so great, a constellation was named after him (modern stargazers call the constellation Cygnus—the swan—a tribute to Orpheus' last song).

To the right of Orpheus is the constellation Lyra, the lyre. Below these two is a third constellation (Aquila, the eagle). Taken together and marked by a single bright star in each, these constellations form the Summer Triangle, "summer" because the triangle is visible in the summer months.

Thursday night was the seasonal debut of the Triangle. Orpheus must have been hitting on all seven strings because the wind and the cold of previous weeks had all laid down, "even the billows of the sea." In fact, Thursday was one of the hottest, stillest evenings any of us could remember. 5:30 PM notched the mercury at 100 degrees Fahrenheit without so much as a baby's breath to ruffle our plans (Jailhouse to Kayak Kamp and back).

Typically deserted, Jailhouse was littered with beachgoers. Not counting us (Sam, Wild Bill, Danny, SF Dave, StarMan, his son Andy, and me) 20 people were on the beach, which is 20 more than we usually rub elbows with. The bay, on the other hand, usually rife with life, was like the night before Christmas . . . not a creature was stirring.

The only things churning up the bay were boats . . . a couple fishing boats, three or four ferries, and the odd assortment of pleasure craft. We even saw two jet skis kicking up big rooster tails. This shouldn't've been because jet skis, according to Danny, are outlawed for personal use on Marin County waters. Not all of us agreed with him, but after a quick post-paddle Google, Danny found reference to a July 2002 California Court of Appeals ruling that upheld a Marin ban of personal watercraft. Now you know.

Five of us are paddling singles; Danny and I are paddling a spiffy new double. The boat belongs to StarMan, but since he wanted to paddle my Mariner and Danny liked the idea of not having to lug his own boat across the Richmond-San Rafael bridge, he and I team up. StarMan assures us before leaving Jailhouse that the boat cannot be tipped over, and Danny and I discover it is, indeed, as stable as the Titanic, our pod's benchmark for stability.

For most of the paddle, the water makes no overt moves to take the boat away from us. That's good. Then a strange thing happens on our way to dinner on Angel Island.

We're not sure where they came from—maybe from a passing ferry—but steep waves start to build up behind us at the mouth of Raccoon Straits. Then the waves start to break. The whole time, Danny's saying, "Lookit this wouldcha, the waves can't catch us, we're going that fast!"

We are going at a good clip, but I think Danny's in denial because those waves are catching us. Sooner than later, they grab hold of our stern and lift us up. We're paddling like crazy, but the long boat starts to broach, the stern sweeping around trying to slap the bow.

StarMan's double has a rudder. I haven't paddled a ruddered boat in a while, but I figure now is a good time to use it. We're broaching to the right, so I push the rudder all the way in the opposite direction to counter the drift. The boat doesn't straighten out, but it doesn't tip over, either. It just gets swept along sideways with the wave, lickety-split in the direction of Kayak Kamp. This is good. Not upsetting at all.

I think Danny and I are a pretty good team, but during dinner at Kayak Kamp, I hear him tell Wild Bill that my paddle swacked his paddle a few too many times for comfort (Danny was up front in the captain's seat and I was in the outback). To make a long tale short, Wild Bill paddles back to Jailhouse with Danny in the double and I'm banned to Wild Bill's boat.

If the truth be known, I never meant to hit Danny's paddle. I was aiming for his ears.

Stats

Date: 26 June 03.
Distance: Thirteen point zero two six nautical miles.
Speed: Two point six one knots.
Time: Five hours.
Spray factor: 0.
Dessert: Pan-fried mahi mahi cubes shishkabobed between dried apricots, courtesy of Sam's culinary talents. At the end of my second week of a sugar-free diet, the mahi mahi was just the dessert the dietician ordered. Though I've tumbled off the wagon more than once, I did manage to dislodge 6-7 pounds. If you're interested, the name of my diet is The South Beach Diet. I chose this diet because it had the word "beach" in it. My next diet will be The Get Rich Quick Diet. I hope it works, too.

23. Aphelion

About as bad as it got Thursday was Will's no-show at Buck's. Will's never paddled with us and probably never will. But that's not important. What is important is this: Will's the guy who opens and closes the little tavern at Buck's.

We (Sam, Danny, and I) figure a pre-paddle beer on a warm afternoon can do no harm, so we mosey across the dirt parking lot to the wood tavern after prepping the boats. Two guys sitting out front say, "You better hurry, they're closing up early." "They" is a young kid I've never seen before who's subbing for Will and is in a hurry to make dust on the exit road. He's got the key in the door, but obliges our request for a couple cold ones before leaving.

Sitting in the shade of the front overhang on a faded-to-gray plywood platform, we're sipping our beers when Now-'n-Again Ben shows up. No kayak on top of his car. No gear anywhere.

"What's up? Where's your stuff?"

"Can't kayak tonight," he says.

"How come?" we say.

"Got to get together some info for a potential job in India," he says, "and I'm taking Peter out for his birthday dinner."

"How old is he?"

I forget what Now-'n-Again tells us, but his son's old enough to carbon-date Ben. (You can hide your wrinkles, but you can't hide your kid.)

"Whenya gonna find out about the job?"

"Sometime tomorrow, Friday."

"If you get it, when you have to be in India?"

"Saturday."

"This Saturday?"

"Yeah."

Life in the fast lane.

Before Ben's contrail of brown dust settles over the parking lot, we put into a wrinkle-free Gallinas Creek, head out into San Pablo Bay, and set a southerly course for China Camp.

It's pretty idyllic out there. The sky's a deep blue, the water's as smooth as Ari Fleisher's political spin, the tule grass is tall and green, and the wind slips by as smooth as Southern Comfort. Neat.

After a brief safety break in a duckblind close to shore, we round the point just before Bull Head and bump heads against some sideshow wind and water. The two look mean and aggressive, but they're only an act, all carnival bluster. The wind doesn't blow in more than one direction at a time and the waves are orthodontically perfect, all the same height and evenly spaced apart.

We ride this carnival atmosphere out to The Sisters, play around in the chop, and paddle through a horde of pelicans who're practicing their boardwalk routines on the ladies. The big birds are as nonplussed by our presence as the stone-faced Sisters and go about their high-powered dives, soaring glides, and Blue-Angel formations oblivious to us.

Though we're not asked to, we leave, figuring the birds want to rehearse their fly-by-night act in private. Sam suggests we dine on Rat Island—it has a small beach that faces west and catches the last of evening sunlight—and that's where we head. On the way, we take a short educational detour to China Camp Beach where a replica of a late-1800s Chinese shrimping junk is under construction.

Two fellows who're working on the junk are still there. They tell us the boat is being made by six or so volunteers under the direction of the National Park Service and the San Francisco Maritime Museum. Everything is handmade, including the nails. These are made by laying a rod over coals, heating a section red hot, hammering it flat on an anvil, then snapping the new nail off on the anvil's edge. The freshly cut nails are coated with linseed oil, then the oil is burned off. The linseed oil's residue keeps the nails from rusting in salt water.

These nails help hold the boat's wood skeleton together, most of which is redwood. Typically, redwood wouldn't be the best choice because it's so soft, but during China Camp's heyday, redwood was considered "trash wood" and the only timber the Chinese fishermen were allowed to buy.

It's a short yak from the beach to Rat. Dinner on the island's delightful, Sam continuing his chefly ways by pan-frying a small school of ahi tuna in a sauce of freshly picked apricots. Very tasty. Except for an enclave of scholarly herons—bookish heads hunched between narrow shoulders, all clad in dark overcoats and quietly mumbling to themselves—we have the little island to ourselves.

We would've stayed on Rat longer, but after the sun disappears behind Big Rock Ridge in Novato, a bone-rattling chill sets in. We should've expected it: tomorrow—July 4—is the farthest the earth'll get from the sun all year.

To warm up, we wrap ourselves in the kayaks, sealing our body heat inside with sprayskirts stretched tight over cockpit openings. Snug as bugs in watertight rugs, we paddle back to Buck's, stopping every so often to watch the eager folks in the East Bay practice their fireworks for tomorrow night's big show.

Stats

Date: Thursday, 3 July 03.
Distance: To the end of the boardwalk and back.
Speed: One point three zero two knots.
Time: Four hours.
Spray factor: Showy.
Dessert: A bag of thumbnail-sized, cherry-filled sandwich cookies. Since the cookies are so small and the bag so big (mostly air), I eat all I want without fear of overdosing on sugar.

.

24. One for the Record Books

We've been called an eating group with a kayaking disorder. It's a sticky label we're proud to wear; it's also pretty accurate. Given the caloric drift of the group, it's not often we notch the history books with noteworthy achievements. Thursday was different.

When I pull into the parking lot at Point Richmond's Ferry Point, Danny's already there. But his kayak isn't. That's ok. Danny's back's been AWOL, and he's taken a few days off to mend. He and I sit on the top rung of a low fence separating the small square of asphalt parking lot from the park, sip beer, and talk about the maladies of growing old.

Back aches, irritable bowel syndrome, hemorrhoids, skin cancers, incontinence, disappearing hair, creaky joints, insomnia, tendonitis, flatulence . . . We figure we've got them all covered. Then Sam pulls up, and we realize we've forgotten one of the Big Ones.

Though a different make and model, Sam's car closely resembles Danny's tonight: there's no kayak on top.

"Hey, Sam, where's your boat?"

Sam stares at the top of his car. A queer look rolls across his face like a dense fog over San Francisco Bay. "Oh jeez!" or some such expletive. "I got so wrapped up bagging the food for tonight's paddle, I forgot to bring the boat."

Yup, Danny and I missed a Big One: CRS, or Can't Remember Shi_.

Like Lance Armstrong in the Tour d' France, it'll be Sam's name that gets carved into the record books. And that's as it should be. No one can ever steal away his moment of glory. But like Armstrong, let's not forget the talented team of domestiques that made all this possible for Sam. After all, without us, he'd have no one to cook for.

While we celebrate Sam's feat with a beer or two, Kayak-'n-Ken and Brian (a friend of Danny's) arrive for the paddle. They're so impressed with Sam's accomplishment, they keep a respectful distance—carefully avoiding eye contact with him—till they can launch out of the point.

Sam's on a high and volunteers to reclaim his boat from the dark hole of CRS. He'll launch from Jailhouse on the other side of the bay closer to home and meet us at Red Rock.

Kayak-'n-Ken, Brian, and I ride a moderate flood beefed up by southerly tailwinds to Red Rock. We're there in less than an hour and have time to spare before Sam's arrival. Kayak-'n-Ken's spent most of his life on the bay and knows just about everything there is to know about Red Rock. But he doesn't know about the secret tunnel.

The secret tunnel is at the end of an old manganese mine shaft on the island's west side. You have to squirm through a size 6 opening between fallen rock to enter. The last time I was close to a size 6, it was my junior-high-school prom date. Kayak-'n-Ken's shoulders have never seen single digits, but we both manage to squeeze through.

A small chamber grows out of the secret entrance's dark side. A black tunnel slithers upward, but it's too slippery to climb and we don't have ropes. We slide, instead, down a slope of scree to a lower tunnel hacked out of solid rock. Very impressive. Kayak-'n-Ken says we must be below sea level, yet the tunnel's as dry as Tutankhamen's mummy.

We venture to the tunnel's boulder-strewn end. Clear the rocks and it may lead further. But the tide on the outside's still rising and even though the water could never flood into here (we're pretty sure), we head out. The three of us launch from a vanishing beach and paddle 100 yards around a shallow point to the north side of the rock facing the Richmond-San Rafael Bridge.

Kayak-'n-Ken's got his kitchen set up and perking when Sam arrives. Sam looks at what Kayak-'n-Ken's doing, and he's visibly impressed. Ken's had Thai cooking lessons, and he's preparing a special serving of Thai pot stickers in his two-burner wok. Chopping fresh herbs, adding strange-smelling spices and oils, a splash of coconut milk . . .

Sam doesn't bother to cook up the stir fry that sent him into the record books (I checked the rules, and this does not disqualify the record). Sam doesn't have to cook: Kayak-'n-Ken's meal is melt-in-your-mouth superb.

I taste new paddling records in the making.

Stats

Date: Thursday, 10 July 03.
Distance: Six point zero eight nautical miles.
Speed: One point three five knots.
Time: Four point five hours.
Spray factor: Kicked up a bit on the way back to Ferry Point.
Dessert: Fresh blueberries (about as fresh as you can get from Costco's produce section).

25. Jurassic Mud

Today's put-in was at Gristle's Secret Launch, a few paddle strokes closer to Jailhouse than to Paradise. Lugging seven boats through the thirsty field that separates the two-lane access road from the bay felt hotter than the day's official 102°F, but next to the water, the air's hot shimmer evaporated and the temperature mellowed to 90°.

Except for three single outriggers, we (Danny, Now-'n-Again Ben, Alan, Wild Bill, Sam, StarMan, and I) didn't see another boat till Bluff Point at the mouth of Raccoon Straits. Today's waters were boater friendly, too—weren't raucous at all. Yaking on the bay was like paddling in a pool of Ritalin (r) capped by skies piled up as blue and thick as Marge Simpson's hair.

So where was everybody? Beats me. I'm not complaining, mind you, I'm just surprised. I'm saving my real bellyaching for days when the bay's top-heavy with boats. Then you'll hear serious complaining.

At the straits, the Ritalin wore off. Wind aimed at the East Bay passes directly through Raccoon. Thursday's late afternoon wind down Raccoon wasn't fast and it wasn't turbulent, but it was enough to slap together a few whitecaps.

When it comes to sprayskirts, I'm one of the bourgeoisie: I've got one sprayskirt for winter paddling and another for summer paddling. The difference between the two is the way they hug my belly: the winter sprayskirt is a tight fit while the summer skirt tends towards laissez faire.

This evening I wore loose laissez faire. The low-volume bow of my boat tends to squirrel spray directly at me, the water running off my face, onto my chest, and down to my waist. With the winter sprayskirt, the runoff is diverted to the top of the skirt. With the summer skirt, it dribbles down into my privates.

The shock of that first dribble is intense. It's hard to describe. The best image I can come up with is "a bucket of crushed ice." Picture this: you're sitting in a bucket of crushed ice. If that doesn't chase the goose flesh over and around your privates, you're a tougher person than I am. Fortunately, the cold shock turns to numbness after five minutes and is no longer physically uncomfortable.

What becomes uncomfortable after five minutes is your boat filling up with water. A kayak filling up with water is not a stable kayak. Luckily, the distance from Bluff Point to Angel Island's Kayak Kamp—the evening's destination—wasn't much more than a mile. By the time we scraped our hulls on the pebbly beach, my bum and surrounding environs were numb and sitting in an inch of water, but the yak was stable. Little favors.

Wild Bill lit his stove and began frying up salmon and ahi tuna steaks before the salt could dry on our faces. While he tended the food, Alan filled us in on his recent trip to Kamchatka, a peninsula of eastern Russia next to the Bering Sea.

He and his wife flew from Anchorage to Kamchatka's airport, met up with two Russian guides and several kayaking buddies. From there, they helicoptered to a site along the Zhupanova River, which their guides claimed had never been kayaked. They camped for a week, hiking the hinterlands and waiting for a nearby volcano to erupt. That it only managed to belch out tent-covering ash and puffs of dark smoke didn't disappoint any of the campers.

The next six days they yaked down the river. Most of that time was on smooth water, though several stretches of river were Class 3. Back at the Zhupanova's mouth, the group climbed aboard a cabin cruiser and headed out to Bering Island at the north end of the Aleutian chain. Another six days of island yaking brought their expedition to an end.

Hearing Alan's adventures got our juices flowing, and we set out to liven up Thursday's paddle. Two weeks before (on the night of the Fourth), StarMan said he saw what looked like a wildfire close to Kayak Kamp. In the spirit of adventure, we went in search of the blackened ground, but couldn't find anything, hiking around the hillside in semi-darkness for an hour.

Disappointed, we began our return trip to Gristle's Secret Launch. That's when things picked up. First, I overheard the Coast Guard on the VHF radio report a mayday from a burning boat. They didn't know where the vessel was and asked all boaters on the bay (anyone else besides us?) to look for the flames. The fire would've been easy to spot in the dark, but we didn't see a thing. Just wasn't our night for fires.

But it was a night for fish. Beside dinner's main course of salmon and tuna, a third fish erupted from the water just off Bluff Point and thwacked Danny across the face, fell onto his sprayskirt, wiggled around for purchase, but not finding any, flopped back into the bay. Assault and battery? "Possibly," says my oldest son who's studying for the California Bar, "but you've got to catch him before you can press charges."

If it'd been lighter, we might've found him (Wild Bill's an accomplished fisherman), but it was too dark to find anything. Almost too dark to find Gristle's Secret Launch, too. But we found it . . . found it a little past midnight. Also found a slog of mud at the secret site that left it's mark on us.

When Alan described being helicoptered to the remote Zhupanova River and camping next to an active volcano, scenes from "Jurassic Park," complete with hungry Velociraptors and T-Rexes, invaded the vast open spaces of my mind's eye. When I broke the surface of that thick mud at the Secret Launch, it wasn't the vision of Jurassic critters that assaulted me, it was their smell.

Whenever I go near my boat or my rubber booties, I can still smell those scenes from "Jurassic Park." Makes you wonder what was in that mud.

Stats

Date: Thursday, 17 July 03.
Distance: Thirteen point zero two six nautical miles.
Speed: Two point one seven one knots.
Time: Jurassic.
Spray factor: Only in Raccoon Straits.
Dessert: Bakery-fresh cookies, home-made banana bread, fresh-picked plums.
.

26. Synchronicity

"Synchronicity" could've been the in word for Thursday's paddle:

•A week earlier, Danny says we ought to try our hand at geocaching (that's where you use a GPS to track down containers of goodies once you know their coordinates).

• Jay comes back from a Minnesota vacation a few days later with a GPS unit a friend's given him.

• Then Sam says to me on the following Sunday bike ride, "We should paddle out of Mira Monte Harbor this coming Thursday. A buddy says it's pretty nice."

• I google "Mira Monte Harbor," and one of the first sites to pop up is a geocaching site. It gives the coordinates of a black plastic olive jar, which, among other artifacts, contains erasers, a tiki, a can of Spam, a small can of dog food, arrowheads, a compass, pens, pencils, and a notebook. The coordinates of the black plastic olive jar are close to Mira Monte Harbor.

Seven of us meet in the harbor's scrabbly parking lot at 5:30 PM: Michael, Sam, Wild Bill, SF Dave, Now-'n-Again Ben, Danny, and I. The place parses like Steinbeck: a dry wind panting over a dusty lot, paint on the harbor master's shack blistered from years of sun, a mangy "guard" dog chained to the building's side, bold chickens and ducks that don't flinch at our approach.

That's Steinbeck. What comes next flows out of a lush Michener novel. The harbor's concrete ramp empties into mugwomp green San Antonio Creek, the afternoon's high tide pushing the warm water half way up the gentle slope. Lining both sides of the creek—and as far as our eyes can see—is a thick green sweep of tall tule grass. If the baby Moses had been a native Californian, this is where he would've been set adrift to coo in the bulrushes.

But baby Moses isn't here and neither is Jay nor his GPS unit. Without the space-age prop to guide us, we randomly yak up the first narrow tributary that catches our eye. Thirty minutes up the side channel and we still haven't seen the black plastic olive jar. We also haven't seen much in the way of wildlife: no ducks, gulls, herons . . . you name it, we haven't seen it. Very unusual, this great marsh surely home to a gawdzillion creatures, winged and otherwise.

Now-'n-Again plays pointer to our dearth of critters and scampers up a naked 2 x 6 platform that brackets the channel. He scans the horizon, then, pointing south, says, "There's a million egrets over there," a million egrets being a fine substitute for a black plastic olive jar. Now-'n-Again climbs down to his boat, and we gear up to visit the birds when SF Dave's cell phone rings.

A sign next to the entry gate at Mira Monte Harbor proclaims the harbor closes at 8 PM and that the gate will be locked. If you plan to be later than 8 PM, it says to make arrangements with the harbor master. The harbor master wasn't around, so we clipped a note by his door. "We plan to be out later than 8 PM," we wrote, "and would like to make arrangements to open the gate when we get back. Call us if you need to." We jotted SF's number at the bottom of the yellow slip of paper.

SF puts the cell phone away less than a minute after it rings.

"What'd he say?" (we know it's the harbor master without asking).

"Says he's locking the gate at 8 o'clock, and we've got to be off the property by then."

"Off the property by 8?"

"Yup."

So much for synchronicity.

We paddle back to the harbor in a rush, the egrets left for another day. The harbor master is there, waiting, anxious. Says he's got a date, and there's no time to waste. We have to get moving. Someone whispers—a bit too loud—that he probably hasn't had a date since Eugene McCarthy ran for president, but I don't think that's possible. The harbor master's a nice enough fellow, even gives Wild Bill a couple gallons of gas to pour into his green truck's nearly empty tank.

We leave Mira Monte Harbor, but not before agreeing to regroup at Black Point under the Highway 37 overpass. A boat launch into the Petaluma River and a couple picnic tables sit under the big span. Several of us recently swept up by the Tour de France, we figure Black Point's as good as any place to start the second stage of the day's event. Also an ideal spot for dinner.

The evening's meal's a two-camp-stove affair and not fully savored till well after sunset. Over after-dinner drinks, we deliberate the next stage of our paddle. A small break-away group wants to postpone it until the following week, but a larger peleton of five yakers sticks with the original schedule and paddles out the river's mouth into the bay.

The night air is tropically warm with just a whiff of wind. Very kayak friendly. The water is very much into kayaking, too, anchoring our paddles in place at each stroke so we can push the boats forward against the stationary blades, textbook perfect. And the sky . . . the sky's a compilation of both Steinbeck and Michener, the summer constellations nearly impossible to see for all the stars.

Forget synchronicity. Stick with the classics.

Stats:

Date: Thursday, 24 July 03.
Distance: Maybe a nautical mile or two longer in the second stage.
Speed: Paddled both stages like they were rest days.
Time: Pacific Standard the whole way.
Spray factor: Too nice an evening for that.
Dessert: SF's first mate sent along some tasty lemon cookie cakes. The Delilah of the evening's meal, those chewy sweets cut short my diet, and I weakened, eating way too many.

27. Apologies

I committed an Ari Fleischer (former White House spokesperson) in the last paddle report and pretzeled the truth. I described the water in San Antonio Creek as "sapphire blue." There might have been people nearby sporting blue-tinted sunglasses who thought the water blue, and I'm sure I was just quoting a remark I may have overheard.

After reexamining photos from that evening's paddle (prompted by an email from a kayaker familiar with the creek), I did detect a subtle difference in the water's actual complexion versus my description. Were I to put words to it again, those words might be "semi-thick mugwomp green." The distinction is quite subtle—blue and green being in the same color spectrum—and one which only the trained eye of a professional water gazer would notice.

I also received an irate email from a maritime attorney who challenged last week's implied comparison of Steinbeck and Michener. "Now you've gone too damn far," he writes, "comparing Steinbeck with the likes of a dribble mouth like Michener. Consider me outraged."

I had no idea that the classroom essays of Loren Michener (to whom I was referring), fourth grade student in Caleb, Utah, had worked their way into the lawyers' guild or that her "spittle problem" (that's how her six-year-old stepbrother Tommy describes it) had become common knowledge (poor girl has new braces on her teeth that are way too tight). I'm sorry about the implied comparison, though I do think Loren's use of descriptive color is much better than Steinbeck's.

This Thursday's paddle was far less controversial than last week's. The water was gray, the spitting image of the sky above. The first two hours of the yak rained on us, not a heavy rain and not a cold rain. A warm muggy July rain like you might find in New Jersey or Pennsylvania (but rarely here).

The hour before we put into Gallinas Creek only threatened rain, which was good because most of that time involved sipping our launch fees out in the open on Buck's front patio. A couple locals were there, and the conversation eddied around a major distributor trying to nudge them into stocking kegs of beer. But the regulars felt getting the beer from the keg to the customer involved too many steps . . . just wasn't worth the bother when a simple bottle would do.

From beer, the talk flowed to fishing, darts, and high school reunions. We hung around long enough to learn that one of the guys was flying to Texas the next morning for his fortieth. Whether reunion beer flowed from kegs or bottles didn't seem to matter, he was focused on looking up an old girl friend. As thick as the conversation was getting, we had to thin the ranks onshore and launch our boats before the bay ebbed away.

The only flutter on the water the three miles from Gallinas Creek to Rat Island were tiny Shirley Dimple-sized craters left by the light rain. From Rat, we—Michael, Adam's Dad, Wild Bill, Sam, Zeke-the-Younger, Gristle, and I—yaked another 2.5 miles to The Sisters. The water grinched from Dr. Jekyll to Mr. Hyde between Rat and the ladies. Sam, who usually paddles without cubbyholing himself in with a spray skirt, saw fit to cover-up his open cockpit just past Myrtle, the eastern-most grande dame. It was that choppy.

The Brothers were another 1.5 miles away, nestled smack dab in the ebb's path across the main shipping channel. Would've been an interesting paddle, but arguments for the crossing were tossed aside as neatly as our boats were in the uppity water. While a minority bobbed about hemming and hawing, the majority simply turned around and backpaddled to China Camp Beach.

The Chinese shrimping junk under construction at the beach is coming along nicely. The stern plate and a few rows of redwood planking along the hull are in place. A 20' length of 10" x 10" has been cut and looks like it's ready to be set up as a mast. A local ranger we talked to said the maiden voyage is still scheduled for October.

Dinner continues to evolve into quite the affair. Two camp stoves sizzling at the same time, tonight's main courses were mahi mahi smothered in onions, crab cakes, and sausage. Dessert was bananas flambé and apple slices dipped in melted Ghirardelli chocolate. During the meal, we were lavishly entertained to a kaleidoscoping sky, bursts of distant lightning (no thunder), and streams of shooting stars.

The evening was worth far more than the price of admission (besides, there are no refunds).

Stats

Date: Thursday, 31 July 03.
Distance: Six point nine four seven nautical miles.
Speed: One point two six three knots.
Time: Five point five hours.
Spray factor: Out past Rat Island.
Dessert: Until further notice, Thursday evening is a diet-free zone.

28. Global Menopause

Sudden, out-of-season tearing, winds that scream after sunset, hot flashes in the 100s interspersed with cold sweats . . . the experts claim these are the signs of global warming.

Gimmeabreak!

These are the signs of Global Menopause. GM. The Big Change. It's happening now. For gosh sakes, the poles are melting. Changes don't get much bigger than that.

Want more proof? Have you glanced up at the night sky lately? Seen that big orange splotch traipsing along the zodiac? Eleven of us (Alan, Sam, Jay, Gristle, Arch, Wild Bill, Danny, Michael, Now-'n-Again Ben, JW—our newest newbie—and I) spotted the blotch right around 11:30 PM from Schoonmaker. It was hovering in the southeastern sky (in the constellation Aquarius, if you're interested). Just hanging there, staring down at us.

Only two times in the past has Mars attracted so much attention: 60,000 years ago when it spooked the Neanderthals and 65 years ago when it spooked us Homo sapiens sapiens. Sixty thousand years ago was the last time the planet was this close; sixty-five years ago Orson Wells aired his famous radiologue, "The War of the Worlds" (we are such faint-hearted dummies).

So, what's luring the fourth planet from the Sun back into the 'hood this time round? Me, I think he's cruised by for a closer look-see. Menopause on a solar scale's must be impressive. I wouldn't be surprised if other planets started queuing up for a gander, too. Should make for some pretty interesting sky gazing if you're out kayaking late at night. But don't fret your worry beads over an invasion this time: no planet in its right mind is venturing too close.

With this backdrop, our penny-pincher's dozen paddled out of Schoonmaker against a lackadaisical flood toward Angel Island. The wind was from the north and bumped heads with the flood, "bumped heads" being a feature. Without the contrary breeze, the water would've been the Supremes without Diana Ross, Laurel without Hardy, Burns without Allen, Holmes without Watson, peanut butter without jelly. The bay was quite playful without being belligerent. It was Sonny without Cher.

GM isn't something to muck with, and we were wary of how far to push our luck before conditions soured (I once saw a National Geographic special featuring a black widow spider Cuisinarting her mate after a little hanky-panky in the linen closet—a dark image I wish I could shake).

Despite our premonitions, we rode the flood up Raccoon Straits without incident or safety break and swung right toward the east side of Angel Island, where it was very calm. The lead group—it's confidence bolstered to a foolish degree by the relaxed atmosphere—headed around Pt. Blunt to the island's exposed southwest side. Bringing up the rear, Wild Bill and I radioed ahead to see what was up.

"Alan, this is Scuttlebutt. Where're you guys goin? Over."

"We going to the beach just the other side of Pt. Knox." (Pt. Knox is on the island's west end.)

"Whatever for?" says Wild Bill. "Why not wait here till the wind and water calm down?" (Sonny and Cher had just stormed on stage to replace Diana and the Supremes.)

"We'll get the sunset and great views of the gate and San Francisco from there," says Alan.

"You sure that's what you wanna do?" I butt in.

"We're almost there," replies Alan. "Over and out."

"Out" is pretty final on a radio transmission. Not much left to say after "out." When our little pod finally reached the beach (without mishap), camp was already bustling and the makeshift table (made from two long water-worn beams weathered smooth) was laid out with mounds of food bigger than midden piles in archeological digs. With three camp stoves on the sizzle, the smells nearly overpowered the visuals. The benefits of slow paddling occasionally outweigh the perks of fast paddling, this being a case in point.

The beach was well chosen and lived up to all its accolades. The sunset was splendid, the city lights magnificent, the Golden Gate a wonder, the food never ending. Added to the six shooting stars we glimpsed last week were two more this evening (all part of the Perseid meteor shower). One shooting star was particularly spectacular, blazing a long white streak into the open mouth of the Big Dipper, where it vanished.

Inspired by the celestial display, one of our group chose that moment for his own theatrics, lighting a succession of bottle rockets that colored the sky like a Fourth of July poster. We clapped and cheered, hooted and hollered till it was pointed out that our colorful display was right in line with the Coast Guard station at Horseshoe Cove (if the law came to get us, we decided the patriotic thing to do would be to turn over the culprit; for the record, all of us agreed to this, everyone except Michael).

Our departure time no longer in doubt, we packed up camp and caught the last of a played-out flood the three miles back to Schoonmaker. Buoyed by having survived an evening in the wild with The Big Change, four of us pushed our luck another notch and yaked out to Strawberry Point and back.

It doesn't get much better than this . . . except Gristle's new $uper digital camera did a Houdini when he wasn't looking. There one moment. Then . . . Puff. Gone. Just like that. Vanished quicker than Bruce Lee.

It's a message, of course, straight from the source, straight from the heart of She Who Must Be Obeyed. "Don't get too cocky," she's saying. "My hot flashes have just started. There's more to come. Watch your step, listen up, and pay attention."

We're listening, Mama, we're listening (wish I hadn't seen that National Geographic special).

Stats

Date: Thursday, 7 August 03.
Distance: No matter how far we paddle, there's no escaping.
Speed: Can't out-paddle GM.
Distance: Out by Mars might be safe.
Spray factor: Only when Cher's around to bug Sonny.
Dessert: If it was there, I ate it.

29. Mad Mark's Castle

Break out the champagne and set the needle in the groove to some good old Glenn Miller dance steps. We've got some celebrating to do.

I'm proud to announce that the Thurseve Paddle Reports have just been singled out for recognition on the world wide web. Yessireee, Big Time Recognition. The commendation is straight from one of the biggest players in the media ballpark: AOL Time Warner.

The corporate giant was so taken by last week's report, their servers emailed an immediate reply to me. Got right to the point, too; didn't waste time mincing words. In a digital nutshell, last week's report was singled out for recognition by their spamming filters. And more than once. Imagine that. What an honor.

This special commendation is one I'll always treasure. It brings tears to my eyes like no other event has. Well . . . that's not exactly true. When I was in the fourth grade, long division with remainders brought tears to my eyes on a regular basis. I just couldn't handle questions like "14 bananas divided between 3 people equals how many bananas per person?" or "$1000 per paycheck taken out for social security pays out how much in retirement?" I'm still crying over the last one.

My fourth-grade teacher was Miss (this was way before Ms.) Jensen, straight out of teacher training. Cute and sweet tempered, she smelled like one of those models in a Sears catalog. All the guys had a crush on her. When I shed tears over long division with remainders, Miss Jensen would stand next to me, put her slim tanned hand on my shoulder, and lean real close, explaining how to work the problem. If I showed understanding, she'd move on.

I cried a lot in the fourth grade over long division with remainders. Miss Jensen would explain how it worked until this cute little dimple in her right cheek would start to twitch. It was like a nervous tick. When the twitching started, she'd shoo me off to the boy's room to wash my face free of tears. Of course, by this time I didn't need to wash my face, I needed a cold shower. But that's a whole other math lesson.

No tears were spilled over Thursday's paddle. Weren't any math lessons, either. The water was like old men slouched in stained couches watching Monday Night football with fries and beer. Shamefully tame. While the bay wasn't much to talk about, our destinations were very yak worthy.

We were eight: Michael, Adam's Dad, Now-'n-Again Ben, Wild Bill, Sam, StarMan, the newbie JW, and I. Launching from Ferry Pt. in Point Richmond, we made straight for Richmond Harbor. Along the way, we passed a number of wide, deep berths reserved for Matson-liner-sized vessels. I'm not sure why we picked this particular berth to investigate, but we did. The berth was like a summer cold, congested with big and small craft, but nothing serious, nothing to get worked up over. Until we reached the end.

What we saw reminded me of that final scene in the "Raiders of the Lost Ark." You know the one: the crated Ark of the Covenant is being stashed away amidst a million other nondescript crates in this enormously huge warehouse. Who'd ever find it in there? We didn't find the Ark of the Covenant hidden away at the end of the congested berth. We found Noah's ark.

At least it looked like Noah's ark . . . a big wood ship with room enough for two of every kind of animal. Well . . . it was BIG. Just like the pictures they used to show us in summer Bible School. Up on drydock, too, being made seaworthy. You could see where fresh timber had been patched into the hull, which was scraped clean and ready for a fresh slather of paint.

I wonder if you can get reservations from Expedia?

From Noah's place, we headed across the channel past Brooks Island toward the Albany Bulb, landfill to the West Coast's finest growing collection of urban art. Ashore at the Bulb, we split into two groups: StarMan, Now-'n-Again, and I going in search of Mad Mark's Castle (reportedly where nymphs, sprites, and fairies come to frolic at night) while the others went to admire the lagoon art.

We found the castle, a yellow brick road leading to a hobbit-sized structure of smooth concrete. We climbed onto the flat roof from the hillside we were descending, admired the tanned sun waning over the bay, then twisted our way down and around a narrow spiral staircase to the main hall. True to the Bulb's enlightened spirit, the main hall's walls and ceiling were fashionably dressed in a myriad of murals, portraits, and paintings.

We hung around past sunset, but the little people never showed. Parsing our time, we worked our way back to the kayaks where we met up with the others and started dinner. Midway through the meal, a presence materialized out of the dark on the fringe of our merriment. StarMan went to investigate. He didn't find any little people. He found the Rabbit.

At least, that's how the lanky, bearded fellow introduced himself. To cut to the quick, Rabbit's a 51-year-old high school dropout from Detroit with a degree in Art History from UC Berkeley who's caring for the final few off-the-gridders calling the Bulb home.

We spent a good part of our remaining time on the Bulb talking with Rabbit. The Bulb's a remarkable place . . . both for its art and closely intertwined history. Close to urban legend, really. Rabbit unraveled it all into a colorful mosaic worthy of a movie. Actually, there is a soon-to-be-released movie about the Bulb. For more on the movie and the Bulb, yak over to this web site: http://www.bumsparadise.com/

I'd tell you more, but I got to get home and work on my long division with remainders. Sandy's real good with remainders.

Stats

Date: Thursday, 14 August 03.
Distance: Seven point three eight one nautical miles.
Speed: One point four one knots.
Time: Five point two five hours.
Spray factor: Zero point zero.
Dessert: Cake from Adam's Dad's Wednesday night b'day.
.

30. Lightning

Cotton, fuzz balls, car exhaust—whatever they're making clouds out of these days—the lightning ricocheting off their pregnant sides was downright spectacular. The sparks were Fred-Astairing / Ginger-Rogering across the sky when we arrived at Jailhouse at 5:30 PM and still jitter-bugging when we got back five hours later.

Mixing lightning with yaking in open water is like tangoing up Rush Limbaugh and Hillary Clinton in a locked ballroom: someone's going to get roasted. I'm particularly troubled by the big flashes because I'm hauling around a pound of lightning rod in my teeth. You know that treasure at the end of the rainbow? At the end of a lightning strike, there's no treasure, just me.

Which is why I was waiting eagerly for Alan to show up for tonight's paddle. He's the guy you want nearby in a storm. Not too close, mind you, but not too far away either. Alan's the Big Attractor: he's got two shiny titanium hips. Given a mouthful of metal or two sleek bionic joints, I'd cut a jagged course for those polished joints if I were a fast-dancing lightning bolt.

Unfortunately, Alan was a no-show Thursday. Fortunately, the bright flashes kept themselves at a distance. Of course, the only acceptable distance is so far away you can't see the light or smell the brimstone, but I'm not one to look a gift horse in the mouth (unless it's full of lead).

Under Thursday evening's well-lit sky, Jay introduced his son Trav to kayaking. Took the boy out on his first bay paddle. Not only were the heavens ablaze with the Goddesses' skywriting, the water was as jumpy as Rush locked in a tight two-step embrace with Hillary.

But Trav handled the conditions like a pro (he also had the good fortune of paddling Gristle's hand-built Coho, which is about as good as it gets). Crunched right through the surly chop like it wasn't there. Paid no attention to the lightning strikes. Showed no fear or concern whatsoever. Which is just the kind of attitude that explains why certain male animals eat their young. Next time out, Trav'll do a lot better if he messes up.

(Note: I tried to find out what animals eat their young at "Ask Jeeves." When he couldn't come up with an answer, he suggested I "Search Local Yellow Page Listings for what animals eat their young." All I found were politicians.)

Fortunately for Trav, once we crossed under the Richmond-San Rafael bridge, the water went flat and he couldn't tick us hungry old males off with his rough-water boat-handling skills. A little ways into this same bathtub water, Wild Bill goes pale and stammers, "I think I left my camera on the beach."

Leaving Trav with his dad (who I'm sure gave the boy and good talking to while we were gone), StarMan, SF Dave, Wild Bill, and I hightailed it back to Jailhouse. The camera wasn't on the beach. No, Wild Bill had left it locked in his truck, foiling the rising tide of an expensive prize. Lucky Wild Bill. On that happy note, we returned to Trav and Jay and set out together for Chard Island.

Over dinner on Chard, our conversation turned to lightning. Some of the evening's bright streaks were accompanied by delayed thunder, but the majority were silent. No noise, not even a low grumble. SF explained that this was heat lightning. (SF recently completed an intensive training course where he's learned to roll his boat like an Eskimo, so when he talks now, we all stop what we're doing and listen). He said that in warm, humid conditions, heat lightning is caused by slowly expanding air that sparks a bolt. But the moment of ignition isn't great enough to cause a sound. Or some such thing.

Hmmmm. Eskimo or no Eskimo roll, I (who have trouble falling out of my boat less rolling it) had doubts. So I Googled "heat lightning" when I got home. Hah! The authorities (none of whom were Eskimos I'll admit) claimed in hi-tech terms that all lightning is accompanied by thunder. So-called heat lightning included. If you see a flash but don't hear a boom, it's because the event's simply too far away for the sound to reach your eardrums.

Following our dinner conversation, Trav and Jay ambled back to Jailhouse while the rest of us set off for Red Rock. Except for construction lights on the nearby Richmond-San Rafael bridge, Red Rock was lost in darkness and a splendid place to watch the night being quietly electrified.

The sky was still afloat with billows of cumulonimbus clouds, which the lightning lit up like the opening night of a fancy Broadway play. During one intermission, StarMan pointed out the teapot in the constellation Sagittarius, which I'd never been able to make out before, but which was now clearly framed between a break in two clouds. A couple constellations back and to the southeast—in Aquarius—hung Mars. But knobby clouds, aglow from Oakland's lights, smothered it from view.

No big loss. If everything stays hinged together, Mars'll be up there for a couple more nights. Certainly would be a show next week if our closest encounter with the planet is highlighted by flashes of lightning. And drum rolls of thunder.

Stats

Date: Thursday, 21 August 03.
Distance: Nine point five five nautical miles.
Speed: One point nine one knots.
Time: Five hours.
Spray factor: Depends which side of the bridge you're on.
Dessert: Chocolate fudge cake.

31. Shark

Trav baited his line with an anchovy, cast it out into Raccoon Straits, then stuck the long, willowy rod in the sand and wandered over to chatter with us. Before we could fill the lad's ear with fish tales of our own, that rod of his bent at the waist like a contortionist reaching for her toes, then sprang free of the wet sand and lunged for the water.

Trav spotted the airborne fishing rod and went after it, catching it by the shiny metal reel before it disappeared into the surf. Had it the spark of life, that rod—snapping back and forth in Trav's hand—might have been running for public office, gyrating like a nervous candidate facing a pod of reporterazzi.

Only it wasn't a group of reporters tugging on Trav's line. Wasn't a bass, halibut, or salmon, either. That dorsal fin 25 yards off shore said Trav had hooked himself a shark. And not just any shark, mind you. If the length of a dorsal fin is a shark's measure, this one was Hollywood big.

The beast stretched the line to the breaking point, then the rod snapped back and the line held fast. Back and forth it went. A strong line when the contest first got underway, we started to have misgivings about it, to doubt its integrity after a time. Maybe we should cut it and let the shark have the day.

Knives at the ready, something interesting happened. Two harbor seals swam close to shore and barked their disapproval of a shark in their waters. The shark, seeing his real prey, forgot about the contest and went for the seals. But the seals were pretty cunning themselves and, through an intricate series of contortions and underwater maneuverings that left us breathless, forced the shark to flop ashore right at our feet.

Prepared just so, shark can be pretty tasty, and the thought of shark marinated in red wine did have a certain appeal. But the final consensus—we have an influential plot of vegans in the group—was that shark marinated in red wine wasn't entirely pc. Agreeing the middle path between a hard line and a floundering shark was best, five of us held the creature down while Jay cut him loose—after a stern warning not to muddy our waters again—and reeled in the limp line.

My mother's always wanted me to be president, but I don't have what it takes. I just can't fudge a convincing tale. And if somehow I do, I can't help but fess up at the end:

I exaggerated about the shark. I made him sound like a big shark. He wasn't; he was a leopard shark, three feet long. Maybe a bit shorter. It was no contest, either. Trav reeled him right in. Took less than a couple minutes. There were two harbor seals, but they kept their distance. And when the shark flopped ashore, he rolled over onto his back and exposed his white belly like a circus seal. I held him down by myself while Jay cut him loose. No big deal.

Our fishing adventure took place at Kayak Kamp beach on Angel Island. Nine of us— Gristle, Zeke-the-Younger, Jay, Travis, Sam, HR, Adam's Dad, SF Dave, and I—paddled from HR's dock in paradise to the camp (actually, seven of us paddled from HR's dock; SF Dave paddled from Horseshoe Cove, but his wife's not suppose to know he did that). Gristle's mate, Helen, took the ferry from Tiburon and met us on the beach. All in all, we were ten campers.

The evening was beautiful, the skies clear until 11 PM, just long enough to spot orange Mars coming out from behind a distant copse of oak to the south. The dew point surfaced before Mars, coating our tents and sleeping gear with a fine wet mist, the moisture soaked up later that morning by a thirsty westerly breeze. Dinner was generous, complete with a chocolate layer cake to celebrate Trav's nineteenth b'day.

And that's the truth (is there still time to get on the recall ballot for California governor?)

Stats

Date: Thursday, 28 August 03.
Distance: To the edge of truth and back.
Speed: Went by so quick, the campout's a blur.
Time: Longer than usual.
Spray factor: Absent.
Dessert: Trav's b'day cake, a particularly fine piece of artwork, the two layers separated by a thick surf of soft chocolate filling.

32. Disconnect

"We've been eating dinners on this beach for years," says Gristle.

"It's against the rules," says the Gen-X-aged park ranger, his flashlight beam swooping across Gristle's face. "Everyone's got to leave the park after sunset."

"Other rangers've let us stay," I say. "As long as we're not leaving any cars in the parking lot, it's been ok with them."

"What're their names," says the kid, his pen poised over a dog-eared notepad.

"I don't remember," I mumble, my memory a jumbled knot of senior moments.

"We had some kids sneak in here a couple weeks ago," says the kid without missing a beat, "and they left one heck of a mess. Beer cans, food wrappers, bottles, paper . . . you name it, they tossed it all over the place."

"You won't find any litter when we're gone," pipes in Michael. "You're talking about someone else making a mess, not us. Morning comes, you won't be able to tell we were here."

"Can't help it," says the kid. "Rules are rules."

Gristle, I can see by his narrowing eyes, is getting mildly impatient with the kid. "Look," Gristle says, "I've been coming to this beach for more'n fifty years. Used to drive down here after school with girlfriends back in the '50s, that's how long it's been. Never had any problems then or now."

I can see it in the kid's eyes. But it's not impatience like Gristle's. The kid isn't impatient. He's plenty patient. He's enjoying laying out the rules for us geezers. Nope, it's something else I see welling up in his face.

It's the same look I see in the boys at home when they bumble across Sandy and me smooching and groping in the kitchen. Embarrassment maybe? That sudden, startled darting of their eyes from us to their feet, like they've just tromped through something. Often accompanied by "Yuck," "Ugh," or "Oh jeez, gimme a break" or some such agonized moan before disappearing into another room.

That's what I see in the young park ranger's eyes now. He's looking at Gristle and imagining him smooching up some high school chickee on China Camp beach. Of course, there's a big disconnect going on in the kid's mind. He's imagining Gristle as he is now, not as he was then. He's not seeing a young kid with a full head of dark hair, smooth skin, trim and in shape, all his fingers and teeth still in place.

Nope, that's not what he's seeing at all. He's seeing Gristle circa 2003, not 1955. Sure enough, the kid's eyes twitch down to his shiny park-issue boots, his jacket rustles as his body shifts uncomfortably underneath, and he mumbles, "Just be sure to clean up," before scurrying off into the darkness to his truck.

Age does have certain perks, and we were left alone the rest of the evening to finish dinner at our leisure.

The reason Michael, Gristle, and I paddled to China Camp beach from Jailhouse was twofold: (1) the last of the flood—and a free ride—was heading that way and (2) we wanted to see how the park's re-creation of a late nineteenth century Chinese shrimp junk was coming along. Last time we were at China Camp, the keel, bow, stern plate, and ribs were in place. Since then, redwood planks had been milled for the hull, curved over a fire to fit, and attached to half the hull.

Curving the planks over an open fire was a close cousin to the technique Gristle used to bend the wood ribs for his two skin boats. A number of folks volunteering to build the junk were still hanging around, and we chatted them up about the planks. It wasn't long before the conversation rambled over to where our kayaks were beached and Gristle explained how he'd bent his boats' ribs in a bath of steam.

Nothing like a shared passion to strike up a friendship . . . in this case, traditional boat building. Gristle talked up Inuit techniques and the volunteers waxed eloquently on late nineteenth century Chinese techniques. A small splinter group—one person—split away from Gristle's crowd and hovered over my wood Tern, explaining that he'd put together a strip-built kayak and wondered how difficult it was to build a stitch-n-glue boat like mine.

We yacked on till dusk, when the volunteers—abiding by the rules—started to amble off. Left to ourselves, the three of us set about the evening's meal. Midway through our efforts, Michael shouts out, "Jeez, wouldya look at that," and points to the northeast sky. He didn't have to point; the object was so bright, it's reflection lit up the bay like neon on the Vegas strip.

Meteorite, missile, space junk—we couldn't tell for sure what the object was, just that it was moving fast, burned purple-red at its core, and trailed a long and intensely bright green tail. In the three to five seconds I followed the object's path, it arced at high speed through 1/4 of the night sky, finally flicking out due east of us.

Had the object ruffled the earth's surface three hours earlier, we might've blamed it for the evening's 3.9 earthquake (coincidentally centered in the east bay); but, alas, the object arrived too late and without any accompanying rumbles and shakes. I suppose a skilled spin doctor could argue that this, the second of two space objects to poke through the earth's atmosphere Thursday night, wasn't aimed as accurately as the first.

But who'd believe that?

Stats

Date: Thursday, 4 September 03.
Distance: Nine point five five two nautical miles.
Speed: One point nine one zero knots.
Time: Five hours.
Spray factor: Zip (not even a small tsunami from the earthquake).
Dessert: Ghirardelli chocolate squares.

33. Heat Wave

We sat in the shade in front of Buck's till it came time to close shop. It was almost 6 PM and still as hot as the innards of a compost heap with no letup in sight. We could've hung out past closing in the shade on the hard wood bench and picnic table reserved for Buck's fancy clientele, but without a source of cold beer close to hand, shade had little meaning.

While Will, Buck's patron de la biere et de l'argente, tallied the afternoon's receipts, we tipped our farewells onto the bar and moseyed across the hot, dusty parking lot to our car-topped boats. We were a formidable gathering Thursday evening, 10 of us kicking up a swirl of dust like Clint Eastwood in "High Plains Drifter" (only it wasn't as hot in 1973 when Clint made his movie).

The regulars were present: Jay, The Shark (formerly Trav), Gristle, Wild Bill, Sam, StarMan, and I. A former regular, Indiana, made a cameo appearance with two new walk-ons, Ellen S. and Steve B. Kayaks were queued up on the narrow dock waiting to launch like kangaroos worrying their turn in the shade of a telephone pole.

The bay was ebbing with a slough of mud exposed between the shore-bound pickleweed and the water in Gallinas Creek. But hardly a shorebird was in sight; I saw one sanderling; that was it. No terns, wrens, rails, herons, willets, egrets . . . the mudflats were a wasteland of life, the heat a winepress that had filtered them out of the picture. More than likely, the birds had stayed home in their air-conditioned nests, the only hotheads on the water us.

Not to discount our intelligence completely, we did take advantage of the ebb and let it haul us south toward China Camp.

On the way, we crossed behind Rat Island where I thought we'd at least see snippets of life sitting in the old buckeye on top the rock. But the tree was as empty of birdlife as it was of leaves. China Camp, however, did offer a glimpse of animation, a great plume of gray smoke etching a backwards question mark over the beach. We went ashore to see what it was all about.

What it was all about was the hull of the Chinese shrimping junk under construction there. The smoke was the airborne distillates of several fires used to heat long redwood planks that, in turn, were hosed down with water. When the right combination of heat and moisture was reached, the pliable planks were twisted lengthwise in a traditional Chinese version of a Rube Goldberg vise to fit the hull's curved surface.

Quite the setup. The process reminded me of something you might've seen in a late 19th century shipping yard (though I've never seen a late 19th century shipping yard, so I guess I don't really know what I'm talking about). But we did see the builders pull one of the just-recently-curved planks from the fire and position it on the junk's hull. The board was a perfect fit.

When asked how they managed to get it just right on the first try, the guy in charge said they didn't. This was the third or fourth time they'd fussed with this particular plank. "Trial and error's the key to our success," he said. You eyeball the board over the fire, fit it to the hull, see where the curve's off, take it back to the fire, and so on. Takes a while to cover both sides of a 40'-long hull with curved planks. If all goes strictly according to trial and error without any mistakes, the builders are hoping for an October 25 launch.

From China Camp beach, we set course for Grindle and Myrtle, The Sisters. The heat hadn't abated a Fahrenheit and the old ladies were zonkered, hardly a ripple at the base of their gnarly hides. Usually, even when the water slow dances past the two, a rave of bumping and grinding goes on here . . . a regular amusement park of waves, swirls, and mayhem. Not today.

The evening's only constants were the gulls and pelicans. Perched high on the ladies' backs, even their numbers had been trimmed to slim pickings by the heat. We would've dawdled longer—been more social—but the aromatic white blanket the birds had tossed over The Sisters was a powerful deterrent to lingering, and we paddled on to Nineteen Palms.

Up to Nineteen Palms, Ellen S. and Steve B. showed they had half of what it takes to paddle with us: they were knowledgeable yakers with sound open bay skills. At Nineteen Palms, however, they proved they had more than mastered the other half of the equation—the most important half, the piece de resistance, if you will. They brought good grub.

Ellen S. uncovered a container of rich, dark brownies I should have shared with the others. And Steve B. assembled his own stove to cook up a cauldron of what he called, "basically spaghetti with egg noodles. I cooked some onion and browned some lean hamburger. Mixed them with some spices and a jar of portabella mushroom marinara sauce. I intended to add some parmesan cheese to it but forgot to bring it."

Didn't really need the parmesan. But it'd be ok if he adds it next time.

The weather being so warm, we lingered a long time over dinner. Midway through our verbal stream of consciousness, a piece of space junk similar to what we witnessed last week—only smaller—fell from the sky into the East Bay, dragging a phosphorescent green tail behind it. When Ellen S. heard about our earlier sighting, she announced she'd seen a news report that Friday about a piece of metal tumbling from the sky Thursday night and punching a hole through the wall of an East Bay home.

Imagine that. We saw it happen (all but the hole punching). Adds a layer of credibility to our paddles. Makes us almost newsworthy. Sound bites can't be far behind (keep your crystal radio sets tuned).

Stats

Date: Thursday, 11 September 03.
Distance: From Buck's to The Sisters and back.

Speed: Mellow.
Time: Five point five hours.
Spray factor: Would've helped cut the heat, but didn't happen.
Dessert: Ellen S.'s brownies.

.

34. Pirate Talk

"Shiver me timbers" and "avast, matey." Also "aye aye" and "ahoy." And best of all, "arrr." We weren't practicing our pirate talk Thursday evening because of the political climate—though it helps to speak the current lingo—but because the next day, Friday 19 September, was Talk Like a Pirate Day.

Another popular pirate term Thursday evening was "grog." Indiana showed up at Schoonmaker with a new 14-foot Arctic Tern he'd just slathered with a last coat of marine varnish. It's an old pirate custom to test the muster of varnish by dousing it with grog. Which we did . . . again and again, cups at the ready to catch the runoff.

You can't just talk like a pirate, you've got to d _ _ _ k like one, too (fill in the missing letters to complete this happy phrase). But don't worry about the order of those letters; it's the thought that counts more than the spelling. According to English taxes put to good use at Cambridge University, spelling like a pirate (they were notoriously poor spellers) just got easier.

The folks at Cambridge in merrye olde Englande claim the most important letters in a word are the first and last. Keep them right where they are, but mess up all the others, and you can still read the word (drink enough grog, and you should be able to read upside down, yo ho).

Me, I tnihk the Egnlsih are jsut mnakig excesus for the islnad's poor spilleng. Wtih tiehr hisroty of pirtaes and big wgis, waht esle cluod you exepct?

The varnish on Indiana's boat still wet with grog, we weighed anchor for Angel Island. In this Indian Summer of global warming, the bay was as placid as the Democratic party setting up shop for the 2000 presidential elections. Not a thing happening. Almost too peaceful, if such a thing's possible.

Even under balmy blue skies on a warm summer's eve, favorable conditions can only be stretched so far. This evening, they went as far as Pt. Blunt on Angel's southeast corner. Before the point, harmony and brotherhood. Past the point, pirates and mayhem. Our septet split down the middle: Ellen, Wild Bill, and Gristle headed back to Raccoon Straits while Jay, Michael, Indiana, and I took on the pirates.

Fortunately, the pirates were just grumpy and not in a fighting mood. They bounced our boats around a bit, tossed salt water in our faces, but by and large were well-behaved. Prior to the group's split, we'd agreed to regroup at Kayak Kamp beach on the southwest end of the straits. They may not have been in a fighting mood, but the pirates did hustle our quartet along at a good clip and we put ashore at Kayak Kamp before the others.

Kayak Kamp beach is equipped with a long, six-inch-wide plank at the tidewrack next to the cliff. When we're not yaking, food and grog are our main forms of recreation. The plank has ample room for both.

Jay produced the first of the evening's main dishes: peanut chicken soup. Poured from a large, clear zip-lock bag into bowls outfitted with spoons (a departure from our usual cupped hands), Jay described the makings as "16 oz. chicken broth, one cup of onions, two cloves of garlic, one or two cups of broccoli/cauliflower, chicken, one cup peanut butter.... and a few other things."

While the soup warmed our innards, Michael put the final touches on a chicken stir fry with veggies. The capper was a secret sauce (I later learned it was Yoshidas Sauce, but don't let on I know). An eleventh-hour addition to the skillet were four links of Aidells sausage Wild Bill was grilling on a separate cook stove.

You can try these recipes at home, but they're best done on a beach. There's something special about the flavor sand, dried bits of seaweed, and pieces of crab shell add to a meal that can't be duplicated in Martha Stewart's prison kitchen.

Ellen, for the second week in a row, stunned us all with her dessert: a whole, as in compleat, berry pie. We bit into that pie and the night sky lit up, bombs bursting in air, and so on. As good as that pie was, we realized there had to be more to this spectacle than sugar and spice.

And there was. This week saw Larry Ellison's Oracle BMW Racing team take on the America's Cup winner Swiss Team Alinghi on San Francisco Bay in the Moët Cup. The fireworks were part of the week-long party.

The light show had originally been scheduled for earlier in the week, but, according to a bit of scuttlebutt I overheard between two pirates, the show'd been rescheduled to Thursday night due to an Ellison gaffe.

The gaffe: the evening of the originally scheduled fireworks, Ellison had anchored his boat just off shore at the beginning of an ebb tide. As the water left the bay, Ellison's boat began to list slightly to one side. Alas, the anchorage the Oracle magnate had chosen was a tad too shallow for the deep draft of his expensive sloop. The evening's fireworks were cancelled so the boat could be rescued (not because of fog, claim the pirates, as the media reported).

And if ttah's not the way it was, you can clal me a pitare, me hearties.

Stats

Date: Thursday, 18 September 03.
Distance: One compleat loop.
Speed: Moderate.
Time: Waits for no yaker.
Spray factor: Ayup.
Dessert: Ellen's berry pie.

35. Paddle Feast

Last Thursday (September 18), sunrise was at 6:55 AM and sunset at 7:12 PM. This Thursday (September 25), sunrise was at 7:01 AM and sunset at 7:01 PM. Next Thursday (October 2), we get a 7:07 AM sunrise and a 6:50 PM sunset. Sadly, it just doesn't add up; we're getting less and less daylight.

But spreading darkness isn't all that bad. Among other things, you get to watch five prime-time autumn constellations steal the spotlight from summer's fading stars. If you live on the west coast of the north American continent, you can see the big five most of the night above the eastern (or just north of it) horizon: Pegasus, Andromeda, Perseus, Cassiopeia, and Cepheus. Take a look next time you're out. They'd appreciate it.

Earlier evenings also are pushing our launch times back. This Thursday we launched from Jailhouse, our last 5:30 PM launch for a bunch of months. Six of us showed up on the long-shadowed beach at the appointed time: StarMan, Wild Bill, Gristle, Danny, newbie Chris Y., and I.

The current was ebbing, and we rode it south toward Paradise. No wind, no waves. Nothing but calm. Figuring we weren't going to find trouble on the water, we pulled up to HR's dock in Paradise hoping to bump up against some there. But loud as we hollered, no HR. Probably out causing trouble elsewhere (residents of Paradise sometimes do that).

Disappointed (HR's also got a heavenly bar), we paddled out of the small cay and back into the ebb. Since I've already groused about it, I won't belabor the point, but it was already pretty dark by the time we left HR's place. We yaked on for another couple miles, then pulled into Paradise beach for dinner just as the last bit of daylight was being sucked off into space.

Ours was a pleasant enough meal, but like the water, it wasn't particularly exciting. Nothing much to write home about. If we're going to talk food, then we have to talk about the BASK (Bay Area Sea Kayakers) weekend party / paddle in Mendocino.

I drove up to Mendocino late Friday morning, which was nice because I didn't have to unload all my gear from the night before. When I arrived at Russian Gulch, the state campground we were staying in, only a few camping spaces were bare of tents, kayaks, and cooking gear. SF Dave had made reservations months ago, so I took one of the empty spots without reservation (SF and his first mate arrived later that evening).

Late afternoon I ran into Indiana and his newly hatched tern on the camp's beach. I had my tern with me, and we were in the water quicker than a great white chasing after a fat seal. The Mendocino coast is difficult to describe . . . sheer cliffs clambering straight out of the water, cathedral-sized caves where the sounds of the ocean enter and never exit, webs of tunnels connecting rock gardens covered with sea life, and on, and on.

Indiana and I paddled three miles up the coast before heading back to camp. New to this kind of coastal yaking, we were cautious, keeping out of the way of turbulent water, not entering caves where swells could enter, keeping our distance from water swirling around large outcrops of rock, and other such maritime worries. That all changed over the next two days.

Groups of ten or more yakers launched from the campground beach Saturday morning. I joined one of them and veered south along the coast. In our group were several skilled paddlers that did all the things Indiana and I had carefully avoided the day before.

Water rushing over and covering a previously exposed rock, then falling away to expose the ragged dome again? These guys paddled up over and then straight down the fluid surface like a waterslide. Tunnels that filled to the top when swells passed through? They timed it so the swell filling up the tunnel surfed them out the other end, thank you very much.

Saturday, most paddlers in our group sat on the fringes of this madness, spectating, taking it all in. Awed. Sunday, we ventured a stroke or two closer to the stuff our mothers told us to avoid. But before plunging into that topic, a morsel or two about Saturday night's feast.

If Saturday afternoon was "White Water Summer," then Saturday evening was "La Grande Bouffe" (or "The Big Chow Down" with English subtitles). Russian Gulch was filled to capacity, over 100 Baskers in attendance. And each one of them prepared a special dish to share that evening. Imagine that. A one-hundred-course dinner.

The spread consumed all of five picnic tables. One table was wine only. Another dessert. Salads. Pastas. Barbecued beasts. For the civilized in the crowd, a portable bar (dating back to Prohibition, it came concealed in a suitcase) was available. I had a vodka martini, stirred not shaken.

On Sunday, most yakers were a bit more daring—confident—the previous evening's feasting and drinking having weighed their anchor and set their concerns adrift. Not that everyone jumped into the really big, hairy stuff Sunday. They didn't. But there was a lot more venturing into caves with medium-sized swells spilling through, paddling over small rocks beset with waves, yaking closer to the cliffs, and other acts that would cause a mother to scream.

Past history confirmed by their behavior this weekend, it was understood that to follow either Don B. or John S. into the turbulence was courting disaster. Disaster happens. I found myself behind both yakers. Don was heading for a tunnel that large swells were periodically closing off. John was waiting for the right time to plummet down a waterfall between two rocks.

I chose to follow John, completely forgetting the third option: to get the hell out of there. To cut to the quick, I was rescued with only minor damage to my boat and ego. Would I do it again? Probably, but next time I'd have that martini shaken, not stirred.

Stats

Date: Thursday 25 September thru Sunday 28 September, 2003.
Distance: Irrelevant.
Speed: Inconsequential.
Time: Fantastic.
Spray factor: Enormous at times.
Dessert: Hand-cranked ice cream, blueberry pie, pecan pie, peach pie, German chocolate cake, fudge brownies, cookies of all kinds, and other stuff I ate but can't remember.

.

36. Two-Buck Chuck

The optimist, I ignored fall's high five—Pegasus, Andromeda, Perseus, Cassiopeia, and Cepheus—and dressed for a summer-evening paddle: shorts, thin Capilene top, shoes with enough small holes to fill Albert Hall. Would've been all right, too, but I was in the Titanic's way-back and my spray skirt kept billowing off like the aluminum top to a container of Jiffy Pop Popcorn.

Whenever the spray skirt broke free, cold water would splash in over the open cockpit. Onto my shorts. My Capilene top was a water wick and sucked the cold liquid up to my armpits. Water in the bottom of the boat numbed my feet.

A few splashy popoffs into the yak, Gristle and I lumbered the Titanic around and headed back to Ferry Point, our launch site. Gristle had another spray skirt in his truck and this one was a tight fit. Didn't pop off, didn't let any more water into the boat. But the damage had already been done.

As long as I was in the boat, I was fine. With a spray skirt intact, paddling a sit-inside is remarkably cozy and warm. Even when your clothes are wet. Even when the outside air temp is crisp. Your body acts like a camp stove and heats up the small space efficiently.

Everything's cozy as long as you stay in the boat. That's the key. Stay in the boat. Get out of the boat and it's a night atop Kilimanjaro in your undies. Seven of us were paddling Thursday; besides Gristle and me, Danny, Sam Wild Bill, Jay, and Chris Y had boats in the water. The other six were all dry. And they were all hungry . . . kept talking about putting in to shore, getting out of their kayaks, and eating an early meal. It was all I could do to stall.

"I think there's a good put-in the other side of that pier way down there," I'd fudge. "Let's check it out." Of course, there wasn't a good put-in the far side of the pier way down there. So we'd paddle on.

From them: "That stretch of sand over there'll do." From me: "Too many rocks, we'll scrape the bottom of the boats." And so on.

Just before Clark Gable sets Charles Laughton adrift in "Mutiny on the Bounty," we find our Pitcairn Island, a public park between points Molate and Castro, a spot we'd passed earlier in the evening after crossing under the Richmond-San Rafael bridge. The place was rundown, weeds gone amuck, the trees in need of an arborist's pruning saw.

A picnic table close to the beach had a half-full garbage can near by. A prime location with amenities. Not a native in sight, we claimed the table as our own. I'd wrapped a couple Sierra Nevada Pale Ales in a pair of leggings prior to the paddle and pulled the bottles out now so I could wrap the leggings around me. Didn't help all that much, I was still pretty cold.

Dinner warmed me up a tad. First course was ladled out by Gristle, who'd cooked up a crock of black-eyed pea and ham hock soup. Chris Y followed with chicken tacos and quesadillas. The main entrée was a skillet of Cajun cuisine, courtesy Sam and Wild Bill. The two hadn't conspired to the dish, but onsite at the picnic table, they discovered Wild Bill's shrimp complemented Sam's sausage and the meal was born.

Well into the spicy shrimp and sausage, bright white lights sweep across us. Natives with torches? The lights rub over us again. And again. Out in the parking lot, a truck's headlights blink through a slotted fence, its spotlight panning. Busted! Trespassing? We aren't sure, haven't seen any signs.

We wait for the ranger's approach and lecture. No approach, no lecture. When George (we name our unseen observer George) drives off without making contact, we figure he's had doubts about confronting seven shadows in the dark alone. We resume feasting.

Twenty minutes later, the truck and its lights return. Same thing happens, lights sweep across us, the truck idles in the parking lot a few minutes, then departs. This time, we figure George may return with the calvary and we take to the water.

The water's ebbing back to Ferry Point at a good clip, and we don't have to do much of anything other than sit back and be ferried along. Which is why you have to understand about Two-Buck Chuck. The creation of Charles Shaw (owned by California vintner Fred Franzia), Two-Buck Chuck at $1.99 a bottle is the 21st century's Ripple, maybe better.

We had three or four bottles of Two-Buck Chuck lurking on the picnic table Thursday night. Drank all of them. Which may explain why, when Danny says, "Let's coast back," we do just the opposite and hammer to Ferry Point. All the way. No let up. Warmed me up real good, it did, but I still wouldn't recommend it to anyone.

Friends don't let friends drink Two-Buck Chuck.

Stats

Date: Thursday, 2 October 2003.
Distance: Eight point six eight nautical miles.
Speed: One point nine three knots.
Time: Four point five hours.
Spray factor: None.
Dessert: Chocolate chip cookies and a sugar-glazed coffee cake.

37. Klingons

SF Dave, StarMan, and Sam lit out of Paradise like the Klingons were after them.

"Captain, captain," shouts SF Dave, "Klingon warships uncloaking on our starboard side."

"StarMan," says Capt. Sam, "prepare for warp speed."

"Aye aye, sir," says StarMan. "Ready to engage warp drives now, sir."

"Make it so, StarMan," says Capt. Sam with a wave of his paddle.

Whooooosh! Just like in the tv series . . . a blur and the three were gone. Out of sight, out of mind, like they were never there. At the speed of light, they'd've covered the five miles back to Corte Madera Creek before they even knew they were leaving.

Their warp drives were cooking, the three having stowed away enough carbs during dinner in Paradise to sink the good ship Atkins. Had to've burned up every Calorie, too. When the rest of us—Wild Bill, Gristle, Danny, Ellen, Indiana, newbie Don't-Follow-Don, and I—sauntered at sub-warp speed into the public dock at Corte Madera several hours later, a quick scan couldn't pick up the slightest trace of carbo residue. No Klingon residue, either, which was a good thing.

Though the evening's curtain call was a mellow one for the seven of us, the paddle'd started out at a quick tempo for our entire swarm. We were going out with the ebb, good enough but only a footnote to the evening's show. The real action—the headliner attraction—was the wind. And not just an ordinary wind, mind you, but a stiff tailwind.

If the authorities'd been able to nab the blustery character, they'd've tossed it in the clink and deep-sixed the key. The charge? Assault and battery. That headstrong wind was slapping the water around like Ike with Tina Turner. Nasty behavior. Almost out of control. But not quite. There was a rhythm to the wicked affair that whipped up regular sets of surfable waves. Miles and miles of them. We rode them all the way from the Larkspur Ferry Terminal to Paradise.

Were we accomplices to the wind's criminal acts? I suppose in a court of law it could be argued either way. For my own defense, I'd plead temporary insanity. The Wednesday before our windward collusion, I'd yaked on the first day of the first-ever paddle to promote better bay access for human-powered vessels. Our august group journeyed eleven miles from Redwood City Harbor to Coyote Pt. in San Mateo, the course a straight line running south to north. For the entire five hours, the wind battered us head on. Gusted between 15 and 30 knots, it did.

"By trip's end, I was sandblasted to within a fraction of total exhaustion, hardly anything substantial remaining of my sanity, Your Honor. I was weakened, wasn't able to think clearly, and so I succumbed to the lure of a free ride the next evening, all the time ignoring the turmoil around me. But it couldn't've been too bad, Your Honored Personhood. We were, afterall, allowed into Paradise without reprimand. I throw myself at your mercy."

I once saw a James Cagney movie where he argued a similar defense before a court of law. He was very impressive, but the court sent him to the hot seat, anyway. I suppose if the day ever comes when we get busted for surfing windwaves, we'll have to come up with a better defense than Cagney's. But I can't imagine that day coming any more than I can Arnold Schwarzenegger winning the governorship of California.

Stats

Date: Thursday, 9 October 2003.
Distance: Seven point six zero nautical miles.

Speed: 299,792,458 metres/second for StarMan, SF Dave, Sam; slower for the rest of us.

Time: Close to instantaneous for the three; much longer for the other seven.

Spray factor: Whoooplaaaah!

Dessert: I plead temporary insanity: I can't remember.

38. Visited by an Angel

Familiar with waxing a car to inspire a downpour? Historically, this phenomenon's had serious consequences. Here's just one: if Noah's wife Naamah hadn't shamed the old man into waxing his ox cart for their son Shem's wedding reception, there wouldn't've been The Flood. Think about it. Instead of just two of every kind of animal roaming around today, we'd still have three of every kind, the way it used to be.

Here's another cause-and-effect I only learned about last week (a short story is attached, so bare with me). My wood kayak got beat up caving and rock-gardening in Mendocino a couple weekends back. Cosmetic damage, nothing serious. A little fiberglass here, some sanding there did the restorative trick. Of course, one piece of sandpaper led to another and before I knew it, I was refinishing the whole boat.

Sanded the entire yak from bow to stern. Did it all by hand, too. Took a long time. Then I brushed on multiple coats of marine varnish to protect the fiberglass beneath from UV rays. Hand-sanded between each coat. The finish on that boat looked tighter and shinier than Elizabeth Taylor's mug after a good Botox'ing (I understand several Hollywood stars are considering marine varnish in lieu of the botulinum injections).

Took the boat out for this Thursday's paddle. Set it down in the soft sand on Jailhouse beach under a giant eucalyptus tree. The tree was so tall, you couldn't see the top. After putting the boat down, I moved forward to pull stuff out of the cockpit. That's when it happened.

At first it was the noise that grabbed my attention: sounded like muffled machinegun shots—rat-ta-ta-ta-tat (San Quentin just a few yards away, it had a certain rhythmic logic to it). Then the color leapt out and smothered the sound. And most of my back deck. Where the deck had been a shiny, smooth wood brown moments before, it now was a lumpy, opaque white.

Rat-ta-ta-ta-tat. One last burst, then the sound of large, soft wings in flight, and it was over. Noah waxing his ox cart changed the face of the earth; me varnishing my kayak only changed how the kayak looked. But I sense some deeper cosmic cause-and-effect at work here. If anyone else has ever varnished a wood boat and then been visited by an angel, please let me know.

Aside from that brief visitation, the evening was uneventful. None of the horrific wind and wannabe Tsunami waves from last week. The water was as smooth as an infant's backside and the wind just as sweet. Chris Y, Gristle, Danny, and I mused ourselves from Jailhouse to China Camp Beach, taking a long, slow pull around Pt. San Pedro to pay our respects to the Sisters who were just waking up. Not inclined to ruffle our sojourn with their evening stretches, we bid them a quick adieu and ambled the last nautical mile to China Camp.

The big frying pans—Wild Bill, Sam, and Michael—weren't with us and, consequently, dinner was a modest affair: cold chicken, sushi, salmon, a couple sixpacks of microbrewed beer, a bottle or two of wine (no Two-Buck Chuck), and a full treat of Halloween cookies. Though we lingered, it was too early to head back to Jailhouse after the last mouthful of sugar, so we sauntered up the beach to look over the Chinese shrimp junk under construction.

The building site was bathed in lights and had a festive look. A fistful of volunteers was still at work, getting ready to lay down deck planks. Among the volunteers was Frank Quan, the last of the original China Camp shrimp fisherman. Though the peak of the industry last saw the light of day in the '30s, Frank never left. Been shrimping there ever since, still lives in a bungalow on the beach.

We hung around awhile and chatted up the volunteers and Frank, leaving just about the time Yankees third-baseman Aaron Boone knocked one out of the stadium in the 11th inning of the 7th game to send the Red Socks back to the locker room for the final time this year. (Ed. Note: Boone only makes $3,700,000 a year, and no one thought him capable of doing what he did. Just goes to show how underrated underpaid athletes can be.)

The junk's maiden voyage is next Saturday. Due to prior commitments, we won't be able to attend: we'll be kayak-escorting the umptieth annual CHOMP swim in Tomales Bay. It's a lavish affair, and we know that the swim's sponsors will reward our steadfastness with mounds of free food, drink, and deserved praise. It seems like the right thing to do.

In the meantime, I have these words of wisdom for the volunteers finishing the junk: Don't varnish the hull.

Stats

Date: Thursday, 16 October 03.
Distance: Eight point six eight four nautical miles.
Speed: One point seven three seven knots.
Time: Angelic.
Spray factor: Not this evening.
Dessert: Halloween cookies.
.

39. Pickup Sticks

A tangle of paddlers showed up Thursday night to yak: Now-'n-Again Ben, Danny, Gristle, Ellen, Wild Bill, StarMan, Sam, Jay, his guest Jennifer (who works in the office just below Jay's studio and whose boss is Wild Bill's dentist), and I.

Getting ten of us prepped and our boats off the small dock at Corte Madera Creek was like a game of pickup sticks, us working our way through the logistical tangle, careful not to upset the other sticks. With the water receding faster than Trent Lott's hairline, the game had a definite endpoint.

The first of us to reach the creek found five toes of water idling by the dock. The tide wasn't going out particularly fast, but it was moving away from the wood structure. When the last of our boats put in, the water was a thin film over thick mud. Gondoliering to deeper water, the last three sticks off the dock were covered in mud, like hot-dipped chocolate ice cream cones.

The rush to launch calmed down on the five-mile, open-bay yak to Red Rock. The water continued at a slow ebb, pushing lightly at right angles against our hulls, not demanding much on our part to stay on course. Behind us, the western sky morphed from light pink through slate gray, plum, salmon, yellow, orange, crimson, and black. The shifting hues gave us reign to stop every five minutes and admire the colorful dance.

All but four of us, that is. Wild Bill and Now-'n-Again powered ahead in StarMan's double once they hit the bay. Sam . . . nobody knew where Sam was. He took off with the double, but soon shrunk to the size of an M&M, then melted away altogether (regardless of the confectioner's claims to the contrary). Danny was the first to leave Corte Madera and was never in our sights, us assuming he'd head straight for Red Rock.

Which he did. The tide was way out and the island guarded by a moat of hull-denting rock, except on the southwest corner where Danny set up camp on a smooth, sandy beach. He had a small fire going that drew us to the spot like light-starved moths. With ten of us catering the event, the evening's meal was varied and tasty, my favorite courses StarMan's peach tort and Ellen's fudge brownies.

Our meals are hard to top. That said, several of us paddled into a spread this Saturday that outdid our usual faire. It was the annual fall CHOMP swim in the shark-infested waters of Tomales Bay. Gristle, Now-'n-Again, his guest Alisa, Danny, StarMan, his wife Carol, HR, and I helped herd the swimmers across the mile-wide bay and back to the starting point, Hearts Desire Beach.

A clone of Thursday night's paddle, Saturday's water was flat, the wind a no-show, the currents mild, and the temp warm. In general, we did an admirable job sheparding the swimmers. The only casualty was a lone swimmer who swam a mile in the wrong direction, mistakenly following an orange course marker that broke free and drifted away from its anchor rope. A CHOMP power boat spotted him and set him straight before the great whites could take a nibble.

If it hadn't been for the heap of food at Heart's Desire, that swimmer never would've slipped though our ring of yaks. Closer to the truth, our attention would've been on him and not on our stomachs. Two picnic tables jam-packed with tasty treats . . . I'm surprised we were able to concentrate at all.

What set that meal apart from our usual faire? In order of importance (saving the best for last): mastadon-sized steaks, barbecued oysters on the half shell, finger-sized chocolate éclairs, and (drum roll) a bottle of 18-year-old, single malt scotch (Glenfiddich for you label sippers).

Like California's governor, "Ah'll be baaaack."

Stats

Date: Thursday, 23 October 2003 and Saturday, 25 October 2003.
Distance: Out and back both days.
Speed: A little bit.
Time: Excellent.
Spray factor: None of that.
Dessert: Peach tort and brownies on Thursday, Glenfiddich on Saturday.

40. Liquid Gold

Evening light on the bay's become as substantial as a mirage in the Sahara desert. The faster we paddle after it, the further it slithers away. Not ones to overdo the cardiovascular, we've bumped up the launch time for Thursday paddles from 5 PM to 4 PM so we can catch the last shimmer with minimal effort.

Three of us were at Jailhouse at the appointed time: Gristle, Danny, and I. Sam's long shadow slid down the bank with the man and his boat not too far behind just as Gristle shoved off for Corte Madera Creek.

Gristle was putting on the ritz this evening, attending a friend's art opening at Falkirk mansion with dinner and drinks at Joe's, and so was on a short paddle leash. By the time Sam had packed himself into his yak and was underway, Gristle had given chase to dusk and was a faded blip in the distance.

"Ya wanna go up the creek with Gristle or head out to the islands now," I ask.

"Jeez, he's long gone already," says the latecomer Sam. "We probably won't catch him much before he heads back this way."

"So, let's paddle with him back to Jailhouse," says Danny. "Company's company."

"Ok by me," nods Sam, and we paddle after Gristle.

Several ferries pass coming and going from the Larkspur Ferry Terminal, and we take time out to snatch a few mediocre rides. We eventually catch Gristle just before Highway 101, heavy with slow moving commuter traffic, crosses over the creek.

"You guys decided to come this way, huh?" says Gristle.

"Uh huh," we say, adding our plan to accompany him back to Jailhouse, then on to Chard by ourselves. Which we do, yaking another mile or so up the creek, then back to the beach at Jailhouse.

While Gristle lugs his boat and gear single-handed up Jailhouse's steep embankment, we spill dribbles of sunset on the beach before putting in. The sun melts below the horizon faster than our liquid gold into the sand; it's not even 6 PM, yet, and we're paddling in the dark.

A charge of wind's blowing out of the northwest, building up rolling swells we can't see but can feel and hear smacking alongside our boats. Riding high on the wind's shoulders is the first of the season's cold (it'll snow tomorrow, Friday, down by the Golden Gate Bridge).

Launching backwards out of Jailhouse, Sam's boat gets heavily caressed by an incoming ferry wake and fills with water. I raft up with him while he pumps the boat out. Danny, in the meantime, paddles on to Chard, scouting the unseeable waters. Sam's boat dry, he and I follow after Danny, the wind-driven rollers winking his stern light on and off like a trail of cookies crumbs ahead of us.

Sam and I follow the luminescent crumbs like hungry trick-or-treaters, catching up to Danny a quarter mile short of Chard. The tide's been on the ebb for a couple hours, and we thread our way along the shore through a kelp bed of exposed rocks, flashlights hunting out some sand to land on. We find a small patch and go ashore.

With just three of us, dinner isn't as grand when more are yaking. Sam's the main provider tonight, cooking up a fish stew of wahoo (Acanthocybium solanderi) surrounded by the last of his garden vegetables mixed in with a handful of storeboughts. If it'd been just me providing, we would've gone hungry.

I wasn't empty-handed, mind you, my gourd just wasn't as bountiful as Sam's: beer, hot milk spiced with brandy, a home-made energy munch, and a dozen finger-sized chocolate bottles peppered with tiny draughts of delight. The kind of stuff you'd expect for

Halloween but not to stoke your fires for a cold paddle across the bay.

Fortunately, the yak back to Jailhouse wasn't nearly as cold and wet as the paddle out to Chard, the wind and water dying down somewhere between the second and third helping of Sam's stew. At least I think the wind and water died down; after the third or fourth helping of chocolate, it didn't matter.

Stats

Date: Thursday, 30 October 2003.
Distance: Nine point five five nautical miles.
Speed: Two point one two knots.
Time: Four point five hours.
Spray factor: Interesting.
Dessert: Chocolate spirits and truffles (courtesy Danny).

41. Popcorn

Ahhhh, the smell of hot buttered popcorn! Brings to mind greasy fingers and big tubs of the yellow stuff at the local movie house. The diet gurus tell you to munch the little bursts one crunch at a time, but it's impossible not to grab a handful and shove it into your mouth in one fluid, tasty swoop.

Tuesday night at the movies? Nope, it's Thursday night at the dock. The popcorn? Who's got the popcorn? We're standing around Buck's parking lot like popcorn addicts queued up at the refreshment counter, and there's not a butter-soaked kernel in sight. But the smell is there, and it's mighty powerful.

Once Gristle cuts the spark to his truck's diesel engine, that wonderful aroma fades into the sunset like the Cisco Kid and Poncho ("The Cisco Kid was a friend of mine . . . He drink whiskey, Poncho drink the wine . . . We met down on the fort of Rio Grande . . . Eat the buttered popcorn out of a can . . . The outlaws had us pinned down at the fort . . . Cisco came in blasting, drinkin' port . . . They rode the sunset, horse made of steel . . . Chased a gringo last night through a field . . . The Cisco Kid was a friend of mine . . . " Heck of a good TV series; the lyrics, strung together a few years after the fact, aren't bad, either).

Is Gristle popping corn in his engine? Nope, but he is running sticks of butter, hamburger grease, cooking oil, and rendered slices of tender pork belly through his carburetor. It's not as cheap as buttered popcorn, but he claims biodiesel drives him to more picture shows than buttered popcorn. I doubt that, but sniffing his truck's exhaust is ok by me.

We didn't see any popcorn Thursday night, and we didn't see any sky, either. Golem gray is what it was, colored a shade duller than lifeless. Which was a shame because the sun's been suffering from a severe case of middle-aged flatulence, sending massive blasts of solar wind earthward with colorful consequences.

Solar wind doesn't smell half as good as buttered popcorn, but it does have an up side. If the earth's tilting south—which it is now—the winds kick up geomagnetic storms that electrify the evening sky with a wavering glow like the picture tube of a color TV. Normally, auroras don't wander as far south as San Francisco Bay. But these recent solar gusts and their hyped-up auroras aren't normal.

Thursday eve might've been host to a most colorful show, but we couldn't see the stage through the lifeless Golem clouding the seats in front of us. So depressing was the gray, Sam didn't even bother hanging around long enough to sniff the last of Gristle's biodiesel, less yak, opting instead to soak in a well-lit sauna some distance away at his 24-hour gym.

Sam's departure left four of us in Buck's parking lot: Gristle, Danny, Indiana, and I. Braving the lack of elements—our only entertainment a drizzle that rained on our show all evening—we paddled out of Gallinas Creek into San Pablo Bay. With a short stop at China Camp Beach to ogle the floating and almost completed Chinese shrimp junk followed by an impromptu jaunt around The Sisters, we descended on Nineteen Palms for dinner.

The smell of buttered popcorn still misting my memory, I had a difficult time focusing on the evening's meal. I remember beer and wine, a tray of chip dips with small pita breads, a standby of hot milk spirited with brandy. Clearest was a round of ground beast engulfing a length of sausage labored together by Gristle's first mate. It was better than good, but it wasn't popcorn.

Stats

Date: Thursday, 6 November 2003.

Distance: Seven point eight one five nautical miles.
Speed: Two point two three three knots.
Spray factor: Zero point zero.
Dessert: An illusion of buttered popcorn.

42. Four-Stick Yak

Jay showed up late for the 4 PM launch—he came by just to shove us off, himself short of paddle time—and couldn't find a parking slot at Jailhouse. The only explanation I can ferret out is the economy must be on the upswing. More money, more stuff to squander it on, more loot for street-wise entrepreneurs, more arrests, more overcrowded jails, and, post hoc ergo propter hoc, fewer parking spots at those overcrowded jails.

Don't be fooled by the GNP; it's the GNT (gross national theft) that counts. The good times are back. Yes indeed, they're back. To add a sheen of luster to the truth I'm shining by you, five houses in my very own neighborhood contributed to the GNT just last night. If you're still a doubting Greenspan, leave your car doors unlocked and your garage door open tonight. The truth'll steal up behind you without you ever hearing it.

Speaking of good times, Thursday's yak was a four-stick event. Gristle showed up with two Greenlands, SF Dave with one, and I had mine. Danny and Sam have not yet seen the green light and continue to beat the water with big-eared European-style paddles.

SF got himself a real nice length of spruce and whittled it close to that perfect combination of shape, weight, and forward motion. The unfinished stick's still got faint echoes of shock and awe buried in it, those too-big blades demanding a mighty big sixpack to twist the water aside (from the perspective of my flabby belly, mind you). Nothing a half hour of cutting and hand planing can't correct, though.

SF's stick's only his second; Gristle's is his fourth or fifth, maybe more, I've lost count. A Norseman by birth, Gristle's a born-again Inuit when it comes to paddles. His latest carving's pulled some magic out of the ether, a slice of Arctic Zen.

The stick's so light, you'd call it runt if your eyes were squeezed shut and it was floating in your hands. But light of day reveals it a decent sized piece of timber, not too big, not too small. Blades are angled nice, too, like a stretched-out hour glass with a set of curves I might be able to pull off in Photoshop but nowhere else. The real magic's the peaked ridge running down the middle of the blades' power face. Steadies the blade in the water, but something more's going on, too.

Gristle and I exchanged paddles on the edge of Paradise, and I yaked with his to Private Property/No Trespassing Beach on the Tiburon side of Raccoon Straits. Subtle is what it was, the paddle dipping into the water, finding its place, locking tight, moving the boat forward, the water humming across those peaked ridges. "Om" was the sound it chanted up my hands and arms.

Before I get carried away, let me say that stick wasn't perfect. Not perfect at all. For one thing, it was too slick, finished too fine. Too smooth. My hands had a hard time staying in one place, slipping and sliding around like I was holding onto an icicle. Rubbing a sheet of sandpaper against it'll change that. Whacking it against a couple rocks'll help, too.

The weight . . . I don't know what Gristle can do about the weight. That stick's too light. Anorexic almost. You have a paddle in your hands, you want to know it's there, feel its heft. But that's just me jabbering on. I suppose super lightweight Greenland paddles are ok. I got to be cool about this. Just because my paddle feels like it's waterlogged . . .

Om.

Stats

Date: Thursday, 13 November 2003.
Distance: Ten point four two one nautical miles.

Speed: Two point zero eight four knots.
Time: Five hours.
Spray factor: Another calm evening.
Dessert: SF brought all the ingredients for s'mores, and Sam provided the fire.

43. Thin Time

Gristle showed up with another new hand-carved Greenland stick, but it was Danny who had the Epic paddle Thursday night. Woven together from little itty-bitty strands of expensive carbon fiber, Danny had to short-leash his new Epic to the boat's deck to keep it earthbound.

I'm not a fan of white-man paddles (big bladed and aggressive, they can torque your body's joints into the red zone), but Danny's did pay some heed to the more friendly Greenlands: instead of Prince Charles ears for blades, his were narrower, streamlined, more like the Vulcan Spock than the British prince.

Danny was first in the water and out Schoonmaker Cove testing his new purchase. When SF Dave, Gristle, and I joined him ten minutes later, he asked if we'd just seen a bright slash rip the dark over Oakland's Hills.

"Nope," none of us had, and Danny figured the sight might've been a lingering Leonid meteor grazing the sky. (Wasn't a meteor according to the late-night news, the sleepy-eyed anchorwoman speculating the intruder might've been a hunk of space junk, but none of the local experts were committing themselves).

After that close encounter, Danny disappeared into the dwindling light faster than the UFO none of us saw. Just dipped one Vulcan blade in the water, then the other, over and over again, and was gone. Poof. Just like that, which wasn't like Danny at all. Normally, Danny's a very social guy, likes to hang back and jaw with you: "Didya see the keel on that boat? . . . How'd your ride go

Wednesday morning? . . . Ever hear of tetrahydrogestrinone? . . ."
and so on.

But not tonight.

Me, I figure Danny slipped into thin time. Normal time's thick, viscous, like Br'er Rabbit Molasses. You feel like you're paddling uphill, always wondering "are we there, yet?" Thin time's like a breeze at your back; it doesn't get in your way, doesn't slow you down. Paddle in thin time and you get to where you're going way before you think you should be where you went.

The key to thin time for Danny had to've been that flash in the sky. Danny saw it, and we didn't. That and maybe his new Epic paddle. The combination could've opened a hidden floodgate that coursed Danny onto a current parallel to ours, a current running in thin time and faster than ours.

Makes mathematical sense, sure it does. If Time = Distance / Speed and the Distance is the same (as it was for all of us), then the greater the Speed (Danny's current), the thinner the Time (for Danny). Plug in some numbers if you don't believe me, just don't let those parallel currents cross, you could get shocked.

What it all simmers down to is Danny got to the Golden Gate Bridge way before us. Up to the bridge, the bay had been all white collars and black ties, well behaved and business-like (Is that an oxymoron?). Under the bridge, the water got pumped up, like a take-charge governor on steroids. BALCO, purveyors of the illegal designer steroid, THG, is based here, and I wouldn't be surprised if they dumped the tainted chemicals under the span, accounting for the disarray there.

Rough water and steroids under the bridge whacked our times back together, and we four regrouped just this side of Kirby Cove. A few remnant swells from a high-riding empty container ship dogged us ashore, but otherwise our beach landing was sweet. The entire park was ours, but we remained loyal to our favorite feeding swale on the ground's west end just above the tide wrack.

Our menu featured sushi, lemon-spiced roast chicken, jambalaya, dessert, and a full bar. The evening clear and more than an icicle shy of cold (47°F), we loitered over dinner till the current was gaboling back into the bay at maximum flood. Danny yaked back to Schoonmaker with us in thick time, nothing much out of the ordinary happening . . .

. . . except for a commuter ferry returning from San Francisco that skidded by its Sausalito dock and had to back up and try again. Ten minutes later, the same ferry crept by us heading toward the north end of Richardson Bay. No ferry docks up there that I'm aware of. Nothing but mud flats. Makes you wonder what it's all about, doesn't it?

Stats

Date: Thursday, 20 November 03.
Distance: Eight point two five zero nautical miles.
Speed: One point eight three three knots.
Time: Thinning.
Spray factor: A splash or two under the Golden Gate Bridge.
Dessert: Trimmings from Gristle's home-grown Ghirardelli-chocolate cake and rich chocolate chip cookies from SF Dave's mess.

44. Thanksgiving

Whose idea was it to spiral Thanksgiving down on a Thursday, anyway? Sure messed up our yaking routine, spinning the paddle out to the fringes of the week. I suppose I shouldn't bellyache, though, the holiday having shaped up quite nicely.

Sandy, the boys, and I drove down to my mother's and from there further south to my cousin's to confront the Big Bird. Quite the appetite seminar it was, too: Big Bird, Little Pig, smashed taters, greasy gravy, cranberry jelly, veggies, pies, cakes, and other sweet stuff to tempt and tame the palate. Mixing it all up with family was pleasurable, too.

Sunday mornings're usually set aside for mt. biking, but Thanksgiving tossed its long, greasy fingers around that holy day, too, upsetting the natural order, and five of us paddled rather than pedaled.

Drizzle and gunmetal drab frescoed the day. Gristle, Now-'n-Again Ben, Sam, Wild Bill, and I converged on a deserted Schoonmaker Cove and meandered out onto an equally deserted bay. It surprises me—maybe it shouldn't—that so few folks embrace inclement weather. Bundling up in rain gear and sloshing over hill and swell's quite refreshing . . . a good-natured slap in the face, a wakeup call, if you will. A couple more months of this sloppy-faced slapping and I'll be humming a different tune, for sure. But for now, I'm comfortable with the metaphor.

Lots of birds apparently are comfortable with it, too. So many birds in the water around Angel Island, you wonder why they haven't flown south. But maybe they have. Maybe they're there already, south of somewhere else. Swinging around Pt. Blunt on the south side of Angel, we stumbled onto the set of Hitchcock's sequel to "The Birds" (which was filmed just a couple miles up the coast in Bodega Bay).

Adding to Hitchcock's original cast of gulls, crows, ravens, and white-rumped avocets (I swear I saw one pecking on Tippi Hedron's noggin, though if I'd been cast for the role, I'd have made a winged pass at Suzanne Pleshette), the sequel at Angel included pelagic cormorants, Caspian terns, and brown pelicans. Lots of them. A cast of thousands. Though not as staggering in numbers, pelicans command the greatest stage presence. Compared to other foul, they come across like airborne Hummers.

BTW, whataya say to a pelican heading your way?

Nothing, you duck and cover.

Which we did, returning safely to Schoonmaker some hours later against the last of an aging ebb.

Stats

Date: Sunday, 30 November 03.
Distance: Eight point two four five nautical miles.
Speed: Two point seven five zero knots.
Time: Three hours.
Spray factor: None.
Dessert: Remnants of my cousin's sweet Thanksgiving zucchini bread.

45. Port-a-Potties

Port-a-potties are the new status symbol in Marin. Used to be dumpster dumpsters, the big, battered garbage bin parked outside your home a sign of social ascendancy. But times change. Now, a port-a-potty out front of *la grande maison* signals success.

I lapse into port-a-potties because the scullers' clubhouse next to the public launch on Corte Madera Creek is sporting one of the rigid blue uprights next to its refurbished entrance. It's not just the entrance that's getting a facelift, either. The whole clubhouse is being botoxed into Hollywood grand.

The closest any of my yaker cohorts and I have gotten to a clubhouse of our own is Buck's, and that's not even a clubhouse. But I shouldn't complain, shouldn't let the jealousy show through my transparency. That port-a-potty next to the scullers' clubhouse is a lot more convenient than the big clump of rhododendron it's replaced.

Three of us admire the new port-a-potty: Gristle, Danny, and I. Sam graces us with a cameo appearance enroute to the sauna, but shows no interest in the plastic latrine. With Sam seeing us off, we launch from the small public dock next to the rowing club into a gray veil of tears.

The long, dark corridor of thick fog we're in disappears Berkeley, Oakland, and all of the east bay. We paddle within 150 yards of the upwardly mobile Tiburon shoreline and are able to make out dim shapes, a breakwater here, a port-a-potty there. The still fog weeps on us without letup.

Paddling in a fog is meditative and alters your consciousness, which segues into this conversation somewhere between Corte Madera Creek and Paradise:

"You guys ever buy or sell anything on eBay," Danny asks between strokes.

"Yeah, sure," says Gristle. "I wanted this fedora, but there was only one guy who made 'em, and they cost $300. I found one on eBay and got it for $15. How 'bout you, Danny? You ever bid on anything?"

No, he hadn't, but "I just sold something last week," Danny says.

"What might've that been?" asks Gristle.

"A phone booth," says Danny.

"A phone booth!" chorus Gristle and I, a doubt of skepticism questioning our exclamation.

And Danny explains about the phone booth in his roller hockey rink that succumbed to cell phones, was disconnected, and left high and dry by the phone company.

"How'd you get it to the winning bidder?"

"He drove down from Chico and picked it up himself."

"Why'd he want a phone booth?"

"Said he wanted to use it for a storage closet," says Danny. "Liked to look at his stuff even when it was hidden away. How 'bout you, John? Ever do anything on eBay?"

I'm embarrassed by my single eBay outing, but the fog has altered my consciousness enough for me to confess bidding on one of those S&M (Shock & Maul) dog collars that're supposed to zap wayward hounds into sniveling obedience.

"Didya get it?"

"Yeah, but I could never bring myself around to use it. I've been bribing the dog with cheese instead, and it seems to work."

At this juncture in the narrative, Danny says he thinks we may be getting close to Paradise, the evening's destination. Though none of us can see the shore for dark, we think we agree. I point toward a thick emptiness to starboard and say, "I reckon it's right there," a modern-day Jack Aubrey.

We paddle through the endless drizzle and scrape across Paradise's pebbly beach, hearing and feeling our goal before seeing it. We're all amazed, and rightly so: even in daylight, we've never found our way to Paradise this easily. It's way cool.

Dinner we spread out on top of 3'x3' concrete blocks that keep ferry boat wakes from undercutting the cliff. During WWII, these very same blocks anchored an anti-submarine net that stretched across the bay's entrance. Above us, a canopy of trees gathers the endless drizzle into larger drops that kerplop on our hats. Gristle hangs his stern light high up in the branches for a lantern, and Danny builds a small Apache-sized fire across the span separating two blocks. It's a cozy space, and we continue our jabber over dinner.

I'm sure the topics are rich and textured, but Gristle empties a thermos of hot-buttered rum our way (with a whipped-cream topping) and the rest of the evening really is a gray fog.

Stats

Date: Thursday, 4 December 03.
Distance: Six point nine four seven nautical miles.
Speed: One point nine eight five knots.
Time: Three point five hours.
Spray factor: Not a breath (except ours) ruffling the water.
Dessert: Hot-buttered rum.

Post script: It's not often that I recommend a purchase, but here's a book you should consider for the solstice holidays. The tome, *Hidden Treasures of San Francisco Bay*, is a collection of stunning bay photos. The photographer is Dennis E. Anderson and the publisher is Heyday Books. Especially noteworthy is the San Francisco Bay Resource Guide at book's end. Included in the who's-who list are the Audubon Society, California Academy of Sciences, Marine World, Port of San Francisco, Sierra Club, U.S Department of Fish and Wildlife, and—drum roll—the Thurseve Paddlers. Now that we're a recognized Bay Resource, it's only fitting the subscription price for the paddle reports should reflect our new station in the food chain. Henceforward, the annual cost for the reports is double what you're now paying. We'll take credit cards, checks, Euros, or promissory notes. A case of Heinekens could work, too.

.

46. Survivor

We made the first cut, yes we did. All eight of us (Jay, Sam, Gristle, Indiana, Danny, Now-'n-Again Ben, Joan la Newbie, and I) could stay on the island.

We'd just hitched a ride on a fast-moving but even-tempered ebb from Jailhouse to Angel Island. Yaking under a clear, streak-free window between storms, bay spray rarely rose high enough to sully the finish on our decks. Even the mile-long jaunt from Tiburon's Bluff Pt. across Raccoon Straits to Angel Island's Ayala Cove was peaceful, none of the swash-buckling action that plays sidekick to a ripping ebb stirring up trouble.

Cruising silently into Ayala's little harbor a little after 5 PM, we watch the last set of contestants booted off the island board the ferry to Tiburon. An official white pickup prowls the picnic grounds, bright headlights searching out rejectees who might've slipped back onto the island after sunset.

Figuring our best chance to stay on the island is to go in BIG and BOLD, we land on the beach with our running lights lit up brighter than the Christmas tree at Times Square. Isn't more than a few seconds after we touch down that the truck's headlights latch onto us. A car door slams, and we can just make out the dim outline of the island's official Gatekeeper heading our way.

Staying on the island's all quick thinking, and Joan, la Newbie in the group, pops out of her boat and marches up to the Gatekeeper as Big and Bold as our beach landing.

"You'll have to leave the island," we hear the Gatekeeper say.

"But I'm so tired," says Joan. "We've just paddled from San Quentin, and I need a rest."

"Sorry," says the Gatekeeper, "you can't stay on the island. Those are the rules. You have to go."

"My hands are so cold," moans Joan (in fact, she couldn't find her gloves at Jailhouse and yaked the whole distance without them). She holds up her blue fingers, shivering, for the Gatekeeper to see.

The Gatekeeper looks a long time at Joan's fingers, starts to say something, hesitates, then, "Ohhh . . . all right. You can stay 20 minutes."

We'd passed the first test! And anybody in show business'll tell you twenty minutes is as good as an hour.

Our victory dinner is plentiful with many courses: soups, sushi, shrimp cocktail, fresh fruit, pot stickers, pasta, mahi mahi and winter vegetables from Sam's hot skillet. Buoyant at having made the cut, we offer up a hat trick of toasts: to fast ebbing currents, to St. Lucy's Day (celebrating the bringing of light a week ahead of Solstice), and to Joan's daring-do.

We're about to propose a fourth toast—to a long stay on the island—when a shock of high beams locks onto our raised glasses. An amplified voice declares, "You have to leave the island now." This voice does not belong to the first Gatekeeper. It is not a cheerful voice.

Joan springs into action and valiantly tries to keep us on the island—"But the first Gatekeeper said we . . . But the ebb's moving too quickly for a safe . . ." and so on. But this Gatekeeper's having none of it. He's already made up his mind and cast his vote.

We're off the island. C'est la vie. There'll be no TV commercials for us.

The ebb's running close to maximum, and we incinerate a chunk of dinner calories crossing Raccoon to the Tiburon Peninsula. We danced a fast waltz on the ebb to Angel Island; now we dance a different step back to Jailhouse. Ducking into the fractaled coves along Tiburon's high profile coastline, we do the Eddy-Hop in the backward-swirling currents.

Lighting for the Eddy-Hop is spectacular: a cosmos of stars. For added effect, every three or four minutes the show's producers set off a Geminid meteor to blitz across the sky. Top Gun stuff. But the neatest effect is moonrise over the Oakland hills. A big orange ball fronted by a smattering of long, dark, wispy clouds, it's an Ichabod Crane moon and tugs loose a long guttural of howls from us.

We howl and bebop into Paradise to let our paddles cool and the ebb go slack. The beach is peppered with driftwood, and we add to the pile Indiana's already amassed (he's a natural Eddy-Hopper and danced into Paradise a couple tunes before us). The wood's wet from previous storms, but where there's a will (and a small Presto® log), there's a fire.

We didn't make the final cut on the island, but that's all right. Paradise was nice enough, the fire was warm, and the light show very special. Besides, that island hasn't seen the last of us, yet.

Stats

Date: Thursday, 11 December 03.
Distance: Twelve point one five seven nautical miles.
Speed: Two point two one zero knots.
Spray factor: Another nice evening.
Dessert: No special desserts Thursday night (though Indiana's Double Bastard beer was sweet and tasty). We did, however, spy a 50 lb. box of chocolate in the back of Joan's car, which bodes well for future outings.)

Post script: Your response to last week's request for cases of Heineken beer has been overwhelming. Thank you so much. But please, don't send any more.

.

47. Glassine Window

We paddled on another environmentally friendly, recycled glassine window Thursday evening. Must've been the same between-storms porthole we were on last week—it had that look and feel: translucent gray, dry to the touch, with a wee chill coating it.

Seven of us puttered around in the window's reflection: Danny, Sam, Jay, Kayak-'n-Ken, First-Timer Jonathon, SF Dave, and I. The put-in was Corte Madera Creek, and the take-out was Red Rock, a one-way distance of 3.91 nautical miles. Up the creek and just before the bay was San Quentin, looking quite spectacular melting butter yellow under a pre-Solstice sun.

Less than an hour from San Quentin and under a slowly moving train of stratocumulus clouds, Red Rock offered a handful of beaches to land on. Our first choice was a short stretch of sand on the southwest corner, but we scratched that one due to lack of firewood. SF Dave volunteered to paddle around the next point in search of better pickings while the rest of us regrouped offshore.

Reunited (minus SF), the consensus was to navigate for the largest beach, which faces the Richmond-San Rafael Bridge and is littered with cords of fire-starved drift wood. Rather than taking the shortest course to the beach, we paddled in the wake of SF counterclockwise around the little island.

We didn't overtake SF, but Kayak-'n-Ken did spot his white stern light swinging around the far corner of the big beach. Being a decent fellow, I volunteered to paddle after SF and bring him back.

To whittle a long tale into smaller splinters, I paddled Longshot to SF's Sea Biscuit and never caught up with him. When he didn't see us at the first beach, SF yaked around the rock a second time, me in wheezy pursuit. When I got back to the beach we'd settled on, SF's steed was high and dry on the beach, SF safely ashore. End of tale. But hidden in those rough splinters was a little gem:

The second time at the rock's southwest corner—which had previously been glassine flat—a set of white-topped waves picked up my boat and hustled me around the point, lickety split, free of charge, no questions asked. A real treat for an old horse from an otherwise staid body of water. Where'd those waves come from? Beats me.

With piles of drift wood littering the beach, we forged a respectable fire to squat around, bs, and feast. Sam, fresh from "Master and Commander," cooked up a seaman's pot of salted pork and vegetables. I now know why they called those sailors olde salts. I also know why they were so wrinkled with beef-jerky tough skin, and it had nothing to do with too much sun.

Midway through our eating and palavering, an outboard motor growls close to shore. We ready ourselves for a face-off with Johnny Law ("Building fires in the middle of the bay is a high crime" . . . and so on).

A dark figure steps off the skiff and says, "You the Thursday night paddlers?"

We cautiously nod, "Yup, we are."

"Cool," he says, "I heard about you guys from somewhere I can't remember. Can I join you around the fire for a while."

It's not Johnny Law after all. It's another wayfarer of the night, out cruising the bay to see what's to be seen. What he saw was our fire, and he was drawn to it like a brother moth. A kindred spirit, as it were. Turns out he's a kayaker, been to Red Rock many times, and appreciates a warm fire on a cool evening. We share food, tales, and spirits, toasting the less-than-a-week-away Solstice with the last of the brandy in my flask.

It just doesn't get any better than that.

Stats

Date: Thursday, 18 December 03.
Distance: Nine point one one eight nautical miles.
Speed: One point eight two four knots.
Time: Five hours.
Spray factor: Glassine smooth.
Dessert: Hunks of fine dark chocolate and a round of berry cake (a clandestine exchange of truffles took place between two of us, but no one else in the group is to know about this).

48. Sunday Paddle

Holiday celebrations lit into the Thursday paddle like a white blood cell ingesting a flu bug. When the festivities were sated, there wasn't a trace of the paddle left. By the time Saturday rolled around, I was getting antsy and put out an email to see if anyone needed a kayak fix around Angel Island the next morning.

Given the short notice, the turnout at Schoonmaker was better than fair-to-middling: in addition to me and Trent (my middle-earth son), Jay, Gristle, and Now-'n-Again Ben showed, the latter two close to an hour late.

Seems that Gristle's been running biodiesel in his truck, which is fine for warm weather. Gets a bit colder than warm, however, and biodiesel congeals to the consistency of bread pudding, tasty but hard to digest. Gristle's truck couldn't digest it no matter how hard it tried, so they had to transfer all the gear to Now-'n-Again's car, a time-consuming chore.

That between-storms window that's been popping up each Thursday for our yaks? It popped up again Sunday just about the time Now-'n-Again's sporty red car pulled into Schoonmaker. None of us had ever seen the bay so calm, which wasn't all bad since it was Trent's first outing in a closed-deck kayak.

Trent's a Santa Cruz surfer and says finding a spot in the surf zone on a good swell day is a task. And on a good kayaking day on SF bay . . . what's that like? If it's anything like Sunday, it can be a real lonely place. We didn't see another kayaker the entire paddle around Angel Island. Didn't see many boats of any kind for that matter.

What we did see were hordes of cormorants. The birds were wired for solar, a real lively bunch under the sun, flying fancy patterns over our heads. Long black strings of them cracking the whip, others glomming together and climbing into the sky like cumulus clouds. Regular thunderheads. You had to be there.

Weren't nearly as many, but a small stealth of sea lions and harbor seals dogged us the three miles from Raccoon Straits to Blunt Pt. on the backside of Angel Isle. Just outside Ayala Cove, they surrounded us like Orcs encircling Aragorn's armies at the Great Gates of Mordor. Instead of a cast of thousands, these "Lord of the Ring" wannabes numbered less than half a dozen and were a lot smaller than Orcs. Less aggressive, too; actually, quite playful, the showdown at Mordor followed by friendly water leaps and splashes close to our boats.

The creatures hung around for ten minutes after we landed at Blunt Pt., then took off for more exciting waters when we didn't come out to play. Blunt Pt. beach faces southwest and gave us full-on exposure to the early afternoon sun. We lounged and snacked on the sunny beach till we couldn't lounge and snack anymore. Back in the bay an hour later, long stretches of gray cirrus clouds had moved in from the south and covered the sun.

Another hour, and the clouds had merged into a wide sheet of cirrostratus, the temperature dropping to finger-tip cold. By then it didn't matter because we were back at Schoonmaker, the boats loaded, the gear packed away, and a layer of dry, warm clothes covering each of us.

I figured it'd start storming on the drive home, but I was wrong. The tempest didn't strike till 9 PM and was still shrieking Monday afternoon. For you storm fans, the nearby burg of San Anselmo was mere inches from flooding Monday morning.

May your feet stay warm and dry in the New Year.

Stats

Date: Sunday, 28 December 2003.
Distance: Eight point six eight four nautical miles.

Speed: Two point one seven one knots.

Time: Four hours.

Spray factor: De nada.

Dessert: A tea Now-'n-Again spiced with 50-year-old Moutai, a strong-willed Chinese alcholic brew. Fermented from a blend of sorghum and whatever else is on the barn floor, the warm beverage tasted a bit like sipping whiskey, but with the kick of Sterno.

Photo Gallery

A pod of Thursday yakers pose for the camera (front to back): Jay, Arch, Wild Bill, and Danny.

Pre-paddle warmup at Bucks.

Launching into Gallinas Creek from Buck's.

Danny gets an umbrella assist from Gallinas Creek into San Pablo Bay (the umbrella collapsed before he got to the bay).

China Camp State Beach (both photos).

Kayaks at rest on China Camp Beach.

Nose to nose.

Last of the shrimping boats at China Camp.

Rat Island.

Not much beach on Rat at high tide.

The Sisters (top two photos).

Chard and Buckwheat.

Danny cruises by East Brothers Lighthouse,
now a bed-'n-breakfast.

Big boat, little boat (Richmond Harbor).

R&R on the Brook's Island sand spit.

Bayside gateway to the Albany Bulb.

StarMan and Danny shelter from a storm inside a mural'ized valve house at the Albany Bulb.

Paddling to Red Rock from the north side of the Richmond-San Rafael Bridge.

Silhouettes around a campfire.

The Richmond-San Rafael Bridge from Red Rock.

Dark clouds over Mt. Tam, viewed from Red Rock.

Gristle's Titanic by the public dock at Corte Madera Creek.

Titanic on the bay.

Full complement of passengers.

Corte Madera Creek public launch.

Lost in the tule grass behind the Larkspur ferry terminal.

Commuter ferry heading out Corte Madera Channel past San Quentin Prison.

San Quentin State Prison.

Jailhouse beach.

Four-stick paddle. From left to right: Gristle, SF Dave, and the author.

Setting up to surf a ferry wake.

Bruno's backdoor.

Gristle's Secret Launch.

Wild Bill in chop near the Tiburon Peninsula.

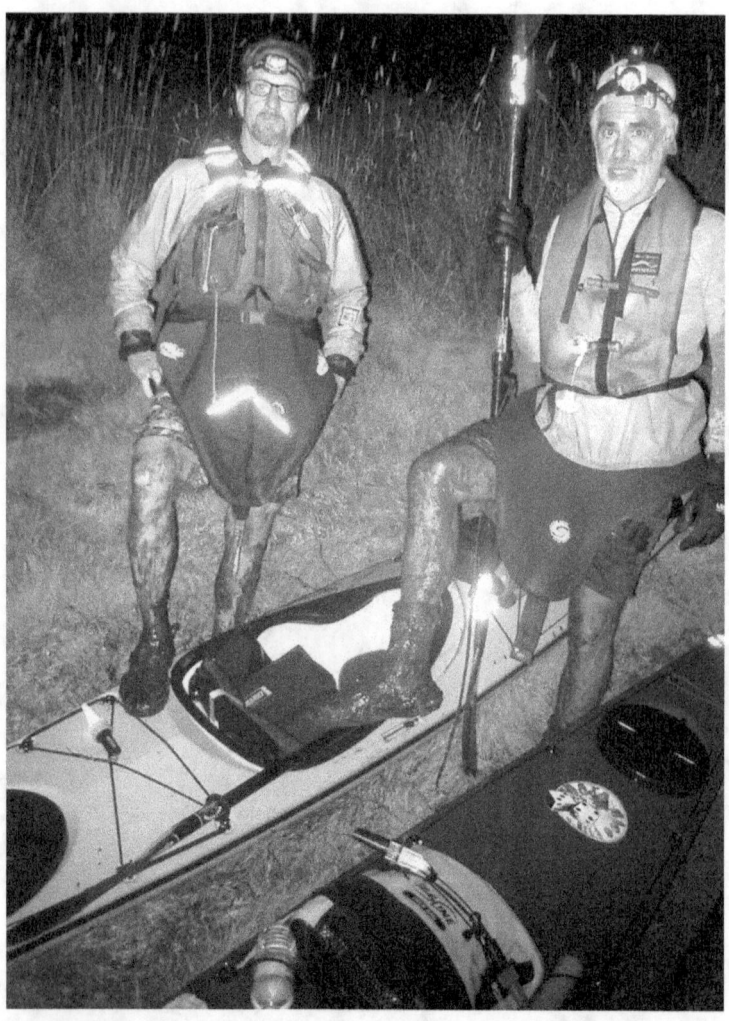

Wild Bill and Danny in low-tide mud at Gristle's Secret Launch.

Private dock put-in just the other side of Paradise.

Sausalito's Schoonmaker Cove.

Heading to Angel Island from Schoonmaker.

Raccoon Straits (Tiburon in the background, Ayala Cove lower right foreground).

Jay hoists gear on his Greenland paddle for the trek to Kayak Kamp.

Angel Island's Kayak Kamp.

Sam nears Angel Island's Pt. Blunt.

SF Dave works to keep his bow up (above) and comes in for a nice landing (below).

View from the southwest corner of Angel Island, San Francisco in the background.

Gristle crosses Richardson Bay.

Jay sits back on a little dumper (above) into Kirby Cove (below) in the Golden Gate Straits.

Now-'n-Again Ben climbs over shorebreak into the straits.

The author reflects (photo courtesy Jay Graham).